... AND THAT'S THE WAY IT REALLY IS!

"Transforming Your Desires Into Reality"

by JACK BOLAND

As Compiled by
Dr. David E. Caldwell

Excerpts from *The Greatest Salesman In The World:*

Copyright Og Mandino, excerpted from *The Greatest Salesman In The World*, by Lifetime Books (800-771-3355).

First Edition

Copyright 1997 Master Mind Publishing Company
All rights reserved
Master Mind Publishing Company
P.O. Box 1830
Warren, Michigan 48090-1830
1-800-256-1984

ISBN 088152-064-0

This book may not be reproduced in whole or in part, by electronics or any other means, without permission.

CONTENTS

Acknowledgments i

Preface iii

Foreword vii

Introduction ix

Chapter I   CAUTION! WINDING ROAD AHEAD 1

Chapter II   OUT OF SIGHT ... OUT OF MIND 5

Chapter III   GOALS MUST BE WORTHWHILE 11
Built-in Excuses ... Not Permitted!

Chapter IV   "ADVERSITY" 15
A Friend in Disguise

Chapter V   THE MIND WORKS
IN MYSTERIOUS WAYS 19

Chapter VI   CREATIVE IMAGINATION 27
What You "See" Is What You Get

Chapter VII   "THE NITTY GRITTY" 37

Chapter VIII   THE IMAGE BOOK 53
A Visual Roadmap for the
Subconscious

Chapter IX   THE LAW OF SECOND FORCE 65
For Every Action There Is an Equal
and Opposite Reaction

CONTENTS

Chapter X	PERSISTENCE	69
Chapter XI	CULLING THE FISH	75
	Weeding the Garden of Desires	
Chapter XII	INVENTORY	79
	A Searching and Fearless Look at Ourselves	
Chapter XIII	DEVELOP AND "HONOR" A FLEXIBLE PLAN	85
Chapter XIV	DISCIPLINE	93
Chapter XV	THE "MEANS WHEREBY"	99
Chapter XVI	ENTHUSIASM!!	105
Chapter XVII	WHAT YOU GIVE IS WHAT YOU GET ... "TO KEEP"	109
Chapter XVIII	FORGIVENESS	117
	An Asset? Or a Liability?	
Chapter XIX	THE MASTER MIND PRINCIPLE	129
Chapter XX	BURNING DESIRE	153
Chapter XXI	INTO ACTION	169
	Let a Winner Lead the Way	

ACKNOWLEDGMENTS

Sincere and deepest thanks to
Dr. Henry Newnan for his continual
encouragement, financial support
and professional consultation
in making this book possible.

Thanks to Wes Fuelling, Linda Puryear
and Cathy Rauckis for their
Editorial Consultation.

Thanks to Steve Yakush and Linda
Puryear of the Church of Today for help
in coordinating this effort.

Thanks to Reverend Guy Lynch
for embracing and supporting the
promotion of this important work.

Thanks to Barbara for her "cheerleading"
and her passion for detail.

PREFACE

There is a dear friend of mine who was aware of the impending completion of my book, and the desire came to him to write a poem in honor of its completion. Now, you must know that my friend never before had written a poem. In the past, he had convinced himself that artistic talent was not bestowed upon him.

Knowing that we must strike out into unknown waters if we are to have the excitement in our lives we desire, my friend took pen in hand and began.

He went into action. The resulting verse was not nearly so important as the realization that he indeed did have a connection with the Master Mind. His intense desire to be of service to God brought forth, through the power of his imagination, the following poem.

Jack Boland

PREFACE

INTO ACTION

You say, "Into action I must go?" Golly! Gee!
But I prefer effort — "effort-less-ly."

You say, "Procrastination will not do?"
But I prefer — just one more day — or maybe even — two.

You say, "It's said that I might fail?"
I'll be safe. Let "status quo" prevail.

"Desires? Goals?" — I would have them as mine.
Maybe I should change. I will — in time.

But time is slipping away from me.
An inner urging says, "Don't you see?"

There is a way. I've just learned how.
That way is — into action! — **Now!**

David Caldwell

FOREWORD

The following was written by Reverend Guy Lynch, Senior Minister of the Church of Today.

I met Jack Boland in 1988. It was clear from the very beginning that he had a particular insight into spiritual principles, an insight that had greater depth than other minister I knew.

In 1991, my wife Linda and I came to the Church of Today to work as Associate Ministers for Jack. Jack told me that I was now going to receive my Masters in ministry. He was quite right about that. I learned more about ministering to other people in that one year before his death, than I had in all my years in ministerial school, and as a minister in two other churches.

I soon understood why the Church of Today had experienced such successful growth with Jack as the Senior Minister. He was an exceptional teacher and leader. He conveyed spiritual principles with a conviction and passion that inspired and motivated people to pursue the most satisfying and rewarding life possible. He enthusiastically assisted and supported people in achieving their goals. It was obvious nothing excited him more than someone's transformation.

There were many endearing qualities about Jack, as a minister and a person. The one I remember the strongest, however, was his personal and caring demeanor. When you were in the presence of Jack Boland, even if you were in a crowd of people, you felt that he was speaking directly to you.

In this book, you are presented with Jack Boland's spiritual belief system. Working the principles as they are outlined will bring you a fuller, healthier and more prosperous life. My prayer for you, dear reader, is that as you embrace the teachings of this book, you will develop a deeper understanding of two basic and very powerful truths — that God is within you and that you are limitless. I lend you my support as you persevere in your life transformation.

As Jack would say, ". . . and that's the way it really is!"

Reverend Guy Lynch
Senior Minister
Church of Today
Warren, Michigan

INTRODUCTION

In this book, you will find many tools to help you change your life ... to change your life in a profound manner. Whether your life is desperately in need of improvement, whether it is mediocre, or whether your life is great already, these tools are guaranteed to make your life better.

In this book you may learn all that you will ever need to know about goals. You will not only learn how to set goals, but you will actually begin the process of demonstrating your goals.

Things that you have not yet believed possible will already be in motion before you complete the reading of these principles. This will be the beginning of an exciting new season of unfoldment and accomplishment in your life.

You and I must always be in movement and in motion. Never will we find a moment in this universe that we can rest. We can pause here and there along the way, and that too, is a part of the principle of life. After a brief season of rest, we must go into action again. If we rest too long, our lives become stagnant and our spirit becomes discontented. Our outer visible experience becomes living proof of the state of our consciousness. We are continually revealing the state of our mind in our everyday experiences.

As of this moment, it seems to me that I have rested too long. I am ready to go into action again. My life is so good that I can hardly stand it ... but it is not good enough.

Things have happened to me, in recent years, that were beyond my wildest imaginings at a former time. Even though my life is full and joyous, more is required. There are things I should be doing, things I have not yet done, and things for me to do that have not yet been revealed to me. I know this is true, that I have to be about this business of getting on with my life.

I cannot settle down. Can you? Of course you can't! That would grieve your spirit. Even though your life might be just as good as mine or even superior, be assured that it is not good enough for you. Proof of the fact that your life is not yet good enough is your quest for new information, new ideas. You are reaching beyond yourself, beyond the experiences you have demonstrated.

In this book you will learn to expand your consciousness beyond your present limits of belief. Then you will go out into your life and prove that **your new belief system is true**.

You will intelligently and wisely set goals that are legitimate, realistic and attainable. I can assure you that there is nothing in life more rewarding and more freeing to your spirit than demonstrating your innermost desires, as actual experiences, in your day-to-day living.

INTRODUCTION

Some of the goals you will set will be major objectives and some will be minor objectives. Each new goal will be important as an integral part of the exciting pattern you are going to develop for your life. Some goals will be day-to-day goals and some will be hour-to-hour goals. There will be goals for new possessions, new activities and goals that affect all aspects of the quality of your life.

Goal-setting and goal-achieving are as natural as breathing, providing you know **how** to accomplish them. In fact, your heart cannot really enjoy life to its fullest, until you are caught up in this process. You are a **natural** goal-setting and achieving entity ... you really are!

Now is the time for you to set that first goal. **Value** must be placed on this goal. I ask you to place this book face down in front of you and take a moment to become still. In your mind, make the **decision** that you are full of excitement about changing your life for the better. Feel the sense of exhilaration you will have when this goal has been attained. You **will** be happier! You **will** feel a sense of accomplishment! **Feel** that happiness and accomplishment, in this now moment, as I take you on your journey to success.

CHAPTER I

CAUTION!
WINDING ROAD AHEAD

Are you aware that there lies within you, a natural goal-seeking, goal-achieving mechanism? In fact, every person on this planet has within them, a functioning goal-achieving mechanism, that is receiving and executing commands every moment of the day.

Why is it then, that so many people do not have the necessities or the luxuries that their hearts desire? More importantly, why are so many people unhappy and discontented? Why do they feel unfulfilled? Why are so many searching for answers, looking here and there, constantly trying to find the missing ingredient that will change their life into one of satisfaction and accomplishment?

Many people do not realize they have a choice in the matter of success or failure. It is a fact, that all of us choose to succeed or to fail on a daily basis. Far too often our choice is, "not to make a choice." We choose not to establish a goal. We choose to go through life as an observer, instead of a participant.

... AND THAT'S THE WAY IT REALLY IS!

By choosing not to set goals, you have actually set a goal. Your goal is "not to succeed." Furthermore, if you have set this goal of "non-success," it undoubtedly comes with a great depth of negative feelings, like worry and self-pity. What happens? The inevitable happens. You stay on the "winding road" and you do not reach your goal. You do not succeed!

If you are not experiencing the things in life you want or desire, the things that will fill your days with a sense of accomplishment and satisfaction, perhaps you have chosen "not to succeed." If you have put off setting your goals "until tomorrow," you have invited into your life one of your worst enemies — procrastination!

All of us have a natural inner urging to move ahead in life and not settle for things as they are. This is a very subtle yearning that at times is barely perceptible, but is always present. If you procrastinate and do not satisfy this inner urging, you will always be in a state of unrest. However, the moment you break the bonds of procrastination by setting a goal, your inner goal-achieving mechanism moves into action. This silent part of your mind acts as a radar system that will lock onto your chosen goal. It will guide you unerringly forward to its achievement.

If you have not given your mind concise directions in the matter of what you want to be, what you want to do, and what you want to accomplish, you fortify within yourself, a state of unrest. Your mind wants to take you

CAUTION! WINDING ROAD AHEAD

somewhere, but it does not know where to go. As a result of this lack of direction, your goal-achieving mechanism becomes "locked-in" to maintaining the status quo, believing it to be your desired goal. Maintaining a lack of direction through procrastination is one of life's major causes of stress and frustration.

Have you ever noticed how good it feels when you have reached a firm decision about some matter of importance in your life? Your inherent powers find it thrilling to have the opportunity to accomplish something for your ultimate good. There is a natural guidance system that is yours to use, and it will always put you back on course as you travel toward your goals.

You go nowhere in life following a straight line. If you say, "I am going to drive straight home from the office," you will prove yourself wrong by the time you pass the second telephone pole. Your subconscious mind is like the steering wheel on your car. Briefly watch your steering wheel sometime as you are driving and you will see it turning ever so slightly, first one way, and then the other. In the same manner, your subconscious mind is constantly making moment-to-moment corrections in your course, as it moves you toward your destined goal. Your subconscious goal-achieving mechanism has become so accustomed to making these small corrections for you, that your conscious mind becomes unaware it is even taking place.

... AND THAT'S THE WAY IT REALLY IS!

Have you not had the experience of your automatic pilot becoming so fully functional that you arrive at your destination and cannot remember how you got there?

If you were to walk across a field while looking down at your feet, you would not be able to follow a straight line. However, if you were to focus your attention on a distant object, your course would become a straight line. As you deviated to the right or the left, you would automatically correct your direction. You would surely reach your destination in less time, and with less effort, than you would if you had not **fixed your eyes on a goal**. Your winding road would become straight. Your path would become clear.

CHAPTER II

OUT OF SIGHT ... OUT OF MIND

Your inner "goal-achieving" mechanism works just as though you were driving a car. To keep from crashing, you must keep your eyes on the road. To achieve your goals, **you must keep your goals in sight**. You will find that it is very difficult to accomplish this unless you **put your goals in writing**. There is a powerful force that comes to your aid when you commit your thoughts and desires to the written word.

One of the world's greatest goal achievers, the well-known anthropologist and explorer, John Goddard, was sharing some of his experiences with a Wednesday evening class at the Church of Today. His story emphasizes the importance of writing down our goals.

John reported the following scenario: "One wintry afternoon when I was a youngster, fifteen years of age, I was doing my homework in the breakfast nook of our home. My parents had invited Dr. Keller, a very successful orthodontist, and his wife over for lunch on Sunday. Everyone was in the kitchen washing the dishes and cleaning up after a fine feast when I saw Dr. Keller

... AND THAT'S THE WAY IT REALLY IS!

wistfully look at me and say to my father, 'How old is John?' My father replied, 'John is fifteen.' Then Dr. Keller said, 'If I could only be that age again. Would I ever do things differently!'"

He said it with such a forlorn feeling that it really affected my consciousness. I thought, here is a man who is forty-two years old and he thinks that life has passed him by. His conviction galvanized me into action. I found a yellow legal pad and started writing goals of what I was going to be, what I was going to do, and things I was going to have for the rest of my life. These were not goals that I would 'like to accomplish' but they were goals that I was '**going** to accomplish!' Each time I wrote down a goal I would visualize myself celebrating its completion. **Four hours later I had written one hundred and twenty-seven goals!**"

John Goddard has completed most of those original goals and has added hundreds more. His life has been filled with excitement and the joy of accomplishment. Some of those original goals were monumental and awesome in their magnitude. Some of them, like milking a rattlesnake or becoming an Eagle Scout, were more along the lines that you might expect from a fifteen-year old.

Some of John's goals were well above and beyond ordinary thinking. How many young men would vow to climb Mount Everest, or visit every country in the world?

OUT OF SIGHT ... OUT OF MIND

John's greatest desire was to travel the entire length of the Nile, some four thousand, one hundred and forty-five miles of primitive, uncivilized terrain. Traveling primarily by kayak, John Goddard and two companions, ultimately accomplished this great feat, and they accomplished it in the face of constant adversity.

Exploring the Nile was special to John Goddard because it was the fulfillment of an "impossible dream." When he originally planned his expedition down the Nile, there were to be five French explorers who would accompany him. Four of them dropped out after corresponding with the authorities of Uganda, Sudan and Egypt. They learned that their journey would very likely be suicidal. The same conditions that had turned back over one hundred previous expeditions were still present and unchanged. The exotic tropical diseases, the raging rapids, the hostile natives, the charging hippos and elephants, the crocodiles ... all these dangers were still present, as they had been for hundreds of years. However, John had learned an important principle about life. You can conquer almost any adversity if you move forward one step and one day at a time. This is the way his expedition conquered the Nile and this is the way you can overcome the forces that oppose you in your life.

John's travels later took him to Central America where he climbed Popocatepetl, the great eighteen thousand foot volcano. Later in this journey, he

... AND THAT'S THE WAY IT REALLY IS!

discovered a hitherto unreported Mayan temple in Guatemala. What a thrill it must be for an explorer to uncover something of ancient history that has yet been unknown to modern man.

What are the odds of John attaining the degree of excitement and success in his life, had he not **written down** his goals at the age of fifteen? I believe that most of those goals would have slipped away and never become a reality. Do you see the importance of committing your goals to the written word?

In 1984, I had the pleasure of traveling to China with John Goddard and there we achieved two great goals we shared. To stand on the Great Wall of China and marvel at the logical impossibility of its three thousand mile length, and to reflect on it being the only man-made structure visible from outer space, was one of the greatest thrills of my life. Later I was even more thrilled to travel the ancient "old silk road" in western China on which Marco Polo's feet had trod.

In 1985, John Goddard and I journeyed to Kenya. There I achieved my childhood dream of being on a photographic safari, surrounded on all sides by the wild life of Africa. Can you imagine my excitement of being so close to lions I could almost touch them, and so close to elephants that I had to look up to see their eyes?

OUT OF SIGHT ... OUT OF MIND

We then went on to Egypt to explore the temples and tombs, standing in the very place where Tutankhamen was buried thousands of years ago. All these things I saw in my mind many years **before** I actually saw them with my eyes.

John Goddard made another important point during his talk. By writing down his simple goals as well as the very difficult ones, he was able to accomplish some of the easier goals first. This gave him the confidence that later spurred him on to greater heights.

You, too, should write a variety of goals. Your dreams and aspirations include all aspects of life. You might wish to find a better job. If this is true, then describe to yourself, in detail, the kind of position you would like to have. Describe the amount of money you would like to earn and even describe the kind of circumstances you would like to surround your work.

You must also define what you are willing to give in return for your heart's desire.

It is very important that you design your goals so they make you stretch, but do not try to accomplish something that is totally beyond reason. Designing goals beyond your reach will only stifle your creative ability by giving you the feeling of defeat. For instance, do not write a goal of being a millionaire within six months if

... AND THAT'S THE WAY IT REALLY IS!

you are presently out of a job and fifteen thousand dollars in debt. I grant you that a few rare individuals will accomplish this feat by winning the lottery, but this is truly not an intelligent goal to set. A wiser course to follow would be to first set a goal of finding a job. Then make it a goal to pay all of your debts. Next, establish a savings account. Finally, set a goal to find a **better** job. Success is often defined as **the progressive realization of a series of worthwhile goals!**

You must act upon your goals. Do not expect to establish a goal of some importance for yourself and then have it miraculously appear without some action taking place. You must do your part by taking those steps that seem appropriate at the time. By going into action you will be amazed as you are guided along the course that brings your deepest desires to reality. Just the right person will come forth to help along the way, or just the right idea will pop into your mind and you will be astounded by your insight. Impossible situations will be nullified with solutions never before imagined!

CHAPTER III

GOALS MUST BE WORTHWHILE

Built-In Excuses ... Not Permitted!

Paul Meyer defines success as the progressive realization of worthwhile pre-determined personal goals. He said, "Success does not come by accident, you can't buy it, you can't inherit it, or even marry into it." I wholeheartedly agree that success is the progressive realization of **worthwhile** pre-determined personal goals.

Now what is a worthwhile goal? I know people who have set goals that have no real value and consequently, after achieving them, there is no real fulfillment in their life. As a result, they spend tremendous amounts of energy moving off into directions that are not consistent with their heart's desires. Perhaps you have set goals like that in your life.

There are unrealistic goals, like the story of Don Quixote who gained fame by fencing with windmills. Even if you win, what have you achieved? Too many people chase rainbows and champion frivolous causes, making "much ado about nothing."

... AND THAT'S THE WAY IT REALLY IS!

It is quite possible to set up a series of goals that really lead you nowhere. We are going to avoid that kind of thinking. We simply do not want to become busy just to be busy, or to set misconceived goals that will require future correction. Why travel down the road one hundred and fifty miles only to discover at the end that you are not where you wanted to be? We intend to proceed differently.

An important requirement for reaching success in goal-achieving is that **your** goals must fit **your** values, **your** standards, and **your** desires. Just as important is the requirement that these goals must be of your "higher self." You will learn to separate these higher goals from the goals that the lower personality would desire.

Every person is a goal setter but he or she may or may not realize it. Most people unwittingly set "negative" goals and then wonder why their lives are filled with negative experiences.

It is important to learn the pitfalls of goal-setting. There are some people who set goals and miss the mark each time, and in this book you will learn why this happens. You will see that some people have the wrong attitude about goals and have set goals **purposely beyond their reach**. In this seemingly innocent ploy, they build in excuses for failure ... for not reaching their goals.

GOALS MUST BE WORTHWHILE
Built-In Excuses ... Not Permitted!

Did you know that such negative goal-setting is possible? If one is not careful, you will set a goal that you cannot reach and then smile and say "I tried, I tried ... I really tried! Now, I don't have to try anymore." This pattern is devastating to your sense of self esteem.

It becomes necessary at this point in your study to take a small but very important action. You must write some goals, and the reason you must do so now, is to give your mind something to accomplish while you are reading the following portions of this book. It is a well-known fact that the mind can think much faster than the speed of reading, and furthermore, the subconscious mind is capable of accomplishing things beyond your belief.

Challenge yourself now by making a list of the things you would like to accomplish, to achieve, to be, and to have, for the rest of your life. Do not attempt to write down "everything" because you will then have an excuse to procrastinate and not write anything. Start by writing one ... then another ... then another. Soon you will have a list, which a moment ago you would have thought impossible.

I implore you to WRITE THEM DOWN! You say, "I won't be able to do them, so why write them down?" Again, I must **insist** that you cannot accomplish them **until** you write them down. They will not become realistic until they are written. You must see them there, in writing, so they will begin to form a pattern that fits your mind.

... AND THAT'S THE WAY IT REALLY IS!

One more thing, write down all the things you would like to do, to achieve, or to have, but also include the silly and impractical things that come to your mind. As ridiculous or as impossible as they seem, write them down. Write them down, even though we have stated that goals must be worthwhile, and we will sort them out later.

As you continue through the remaining chapters, keep a pad handy and write **whatever** desires come to your mind, even if some are embarrassing to you. As a matter of fact, it is **especially** important to take a bold step, and write those goals that may make you a little uncomfortable!

CHAPTER IV

"ADVERSITY"

A Friend in Disguise

There is a story of a Persian prince who was born a hunchback, and on his twelfth birthday, his father asked him what special gift he would like to receive this year. Always upon his birthday, his father, who could afford anything, would give his son the request that his heart desired.

The small hunchbacked child, bent over and unable to rise to his full stature, looked up at his father and said, "I would like a statue of myself." The father was stunned and wished he had not asked. He paused and said, "Son, isn't there something else you would rather have?" The boy, understanding his father's pain, said, "Father, I do not want a statue of myself as I now look. I want a statue that would look like me if I stood tall and straight like you. I would like to have you place it outside my window in the garden. Please place it where I can easily see it every day."

Very painfully his father granted the wish. Each day the hunched boy would go into the garden and there in front of that statue would stretch and stretch and push himself up with every ounce of strength within him.

... AND THAT'S THE WAY IT REALLY IS!

Each day, several times a day for eight years, he would strive to reach up and be like the statue. On his twenty-first birthday, he stood with his shoulders erect and walked into the garden, looked that statue right in the eye and then turned his gaze to look squarely in his father's eyes.

Tears filled his father's eyes as he realized, with pride, what his son had accomplished. Through a supreme desire in his son's mind, he had accomplished the impossible. He did not achieve this all in one moment, but he achieved it stretch-by-stretch, day-by-day. Sheer determination and an unwillingness to quit had produced, in his body, the image that he held in his mind.

If you set your sights for **lofty** goals, I can assure you, your successes will be equally great. Like the young man's body, your life has been misshapen in some form, has it not? Your life has not been as erect and as tall or as magnificent as your spirit knows it can be.

Adversity is good for you! Does this shock you? Adversity is the best thing that ever happened to you, and it will be a part of the process of achieving your goals. Overcoming adversity is the measure of your greatness.

This is a friendly universe and all of life is working to help you move forward and upward. Nothing has been placed in your path that you cannot overcome. There is no "thing" or event or circumstance you cannot rise above.

"ADVERSITY"
A Friend in Disguise

As you begin to move forward into the achievement of your new goals, I promise you that you will find obstacles in your path. The moment you set a goal, you are declaring that you will meet adversity!

The following is a well-known law in physics, and it holds true for goal-setting. For every action, there is an equal and opposite reaction. The greater your goal the greater will be the adversity that will try to keep you from achieving that goal.

Why do you think very few people upon this earth ever set or achieve goals? It is because they do not understand the law. They take their dreams out into the world to experience them and immediately meet with resistance. Then they quit! They quit because they become so aware of the resistance that they lose sight of their dream and focus on the resistance. This focusing gives resistance the **power** it needs to defeat them.

You must also recognize inner obstacles, the secret ones, the silent ones that occur in your feelings. You must not let them disturb you.

If you refuse to let these new inner and outer obstacles deter you from your goal, the obstacles you meet will soon begin to work to your advantage. You will find that the measure of your achievement will ultimately increase in proportion to the resistance you overcome.

... AND THAT'S THE WAY IT REALLY IS!

In other words, the greater the resistance, the greater your achievement will be. What a great discovery! From this concept, we learn an important principle that is contrary to "normal" thinking.

When adversity or resistance comes, **welcome it! Lean into it.** You will meet with resistance and the resistance is good. Within it will be found the seed for the achievement of your goal. **Adversity truly is a friend in disguise!**

CHAPTER V

THE MIND WORKS IN MYSTERIOUS WAYS

After a goal is established, one of our hidden fears about goal-setting is that we will then have to go and do it. True? Can you imagine where John Goddard would be if he had allowed fear of action to control his life?

The truth is that goal-achieving is much easier than not achieving goals. Remaining static is the more difficult choice. Not having enough of the good things in life is the hard way to go. Being poor is a problem that really boggles the mind. That is the hard way to go through life.

"The easy way" is to learn about goals, set attainable goals, and move forward to even more exciting experiences by achieving them. **This is true because your mind is created to achieve goals, and I am saying this to you again and again because I want you to hear it!** Your mind is designed to work this way and it **always** works this way.

... AND THAT'S THE WAY IT REALLY IS!

Now let me tell you one of the most important principles in this book. It is based on the idea that your mind is a goal-setting mechanism. If you do not set goals, the inevitable occurs. **"NOT SETTING GOALS BECOMES YOUR GOAL."**

Your goal is: "I do not set goals because I do not like to change." Your mind hears you say this and says "OK, you don't like to change. Let's settle down right here."

Then we have conflict. Your spirit is always seeking to move but you have settled for nothing. Discontent creeps in and you wonder why you are feeling neglected by life.

Life, however, is rigged to keep you from remaining motionless. In time, your experiences, which are often by this time seemingly undesirable, will attempt to force you forward, out of this inertia. Life will "bang on your hood." It will awaken you and force you to find a better way.

Your Success Mechanism

Maxwell Maltz in his great book, **"Psycho-Cybernetics,"** talks about your built-in guidance system. Dr. Maltz was a plastic surgeon who became a psychiatrist, because he wanted to understand how the mind works. Some of the things he discovered go far beyond the field of psychiatry.

THE MIND WORKS IN MYSTERIOUS WAYS

He believed that every living thing has a built in guidance system or goal-striving mechanism that was placed there by its creator. In the simpler forms of life, the goal is to live or survive as a species.

In man, however, the goal to live means more than mere survival. You have certain physical needs that must be met, but you also have emotional, psychological, and spiritual needs that, to our knowledge, are lacking in the lower animal kingdom.

You have within you, a success mechanism that was put there by your Creator. It is guaranteed to work and guaranteed to help you achieve your goals at every level of your existence.

In man, this success mechanism is not automatic. It must be triggered by the consciousness of each individual. Man is a conscious being who must come to understand the nature of his mind and begin to work with the process that is already there.

To the person who begins to understand, the success mechanism can help him get answers to any variety of problems that might come to him. It can help him invent things that are astounding, to write, to create, to run a business, to explore new horizons, to attain peace of mind, and to ultimately change his personality.

... AND THAT'S THE WAY IT REALLY IS!

These success mechanisms are already working in you. You are not limited to the circumstances that have brought you to this point or to those that exist at this moment.

You have a creative imagination that can envision a future in the now moment and bring it to pass.

How does this work? The word Cybernetics, used in Dr. Maltz's book, comes from a Greek word that means "the steersman." You have within you, a system that will steer you unerringly to a target or a goal. It will do this in the very same way that a missile seeks out and finds its target.

The objective of the missile is to reach a target or a goal. A course is set for the location of the target and the missile finds its way, but not in a straight line.

There is a positive and negative feedback that is involved in the control of a missile. If it is moving toward its goal, nothing happens and it continues to move toward it. The moment that it deviates to the right or to the left, there is a negative feedback and an adjustment is made to put the missile back on its proper course. It does not respond to positive feedback, but only to negative feedback.

Your mind works in the very same way. **This means that persons who are unwilling to admit that they make mistakes cannot achieve their goals.**

THE MIND WORKS IN MYSTERIOUS WAYS

If you establish a goal and then believe that everything you do or think is absolutely correct, there is no negative feedback. The same is true if you are one of the metaphysicians that stand around declaring Divine Order, regardless of what happens. There is no adjustment. No correction is made.

The moment you make a mistake, you can immediately make a correction. These small successes along the way can be rewarding and exciting.

A baby learns in the same way. When reaching for an object like a rattle, it will first miss to the right and then to the left. It finally succeeds by correcting its earlier mistakes. Immediately, it forgets all the wrong actions and only remembers the right one. Through a series of successes it learns to find its rattle and anything else it wants. In time, it learns to fling its pabulum across the room.

You must set your goals, move forward correcting yourself as you go; and as you make mistakes, forget them.

I saw this correcting action occur in a football game. The quarterback faded back for a pass and watched his receiver run down the field about ten strides, turn and then sprint to the left. The ball was thrown at the time of the turn and was supposed to be caught six paces later. The only problem was that

... AND THAT'S THE WAY IT REALLY IS!

the quarterback misjudged the speed at which his receiver was running. The very next play was identical except for a turn to the right. The quarterback corrected his judgment of the receiver's speed and a first down was achieved.

That was a minor goal along the way. The objective, of course, was to score a touchdown and the major goal was to win the game.

Your mind works in exactly the same way. You have within you, a computer, and you are the operator of that computer. There is an infinite store-house of ideas, of knowledge, and of power. Everything you need exists now. You are not limited to your own personal resources. You are not limited to the experiences you have had in the past. You are not limited to the education you have or did not have. None of these things can limit you except if you say they do. If you program into your internal computer that you are limited by these things, then because of that information in your computer, you are limited.

But in reality you are not limited. You are only limited by what you have believed and conceived in the past. You are not limited by your mind because your mind is locked into the super mind. Emerson said, "There is only one mind common to all individual men." He compared our individual minds to the inlets of an ocean of universal minds.

THE MIND WORKS IN MYSTERIOUS WAYS

There is a capacity for applying knowledge that transcends the sensory function, and when you become a goal-setting and goal-seeking mechanism, a very remarkable thing begins to happen.

The universe responds to you beyond your greatest understanding. You have within you, the capacity to draw to you, all the things you need. You can experience all the events, the circumstances, the people, the conditions, and everything that is necessary for the completion of your goal. I know this is true.

Webster defines success as the "satisfactory accomplishment of a goal sought for." All real success is the result of a creative striving for a goal that is important to you as a result of your own deep self needs.

The goals I set for myself will not suffice for you. It is only when you begin to look into your own mind and cause it to begin to speak to you, to reveal to you those goals that are of deepest meaning, that you will begin to feel the warmth of success. When you establish those goals, there will be a sudden peace that will come over you. You will have a feeling of joyous relaxation, very much like getting ready to take a trip you have been looking forward to for a long time.

Remember how it was when you were just ready to take off on that special vacation? Remember the excitement that was there? That's the way it is.

... AND THAT'S THE WAY IT REALLY IS!

You take that deep breath, smile and say, "Here we go." Something is going to happen and you anxiously expect it.

You will find that your mind will come alive when you set into motion, the process of achieving goals. Your life will take on an excitement that you did not dream was possible. Life will be so good you will hardly be able to stand it!

CHAPTER VI

CREATIVE IMAGINATION

What You "See" Is What You Get

How would **you** like to be the creator of your future? In Napoleon Hill's fabulous book, ***"Think and Grow Rich,"*** he writes: "Imagination is the workshop of your mind and is capable of turning mind energy into accomplishment and wealth." He also teaches us that your subconscious or your subjective mind cannot distinguish between what is imaginary and what is real. It sees them both the same. Your subconscious reproduces the mirror image of what you imagine in your life.

If you continue to see your life as it is, then your subjective mind — this powerful creative force within you — will continue to reproduce your life **as it is**. On the other hand, you can re-program your subjective mind by creating images of new life patterns, and it will maintain these patterns **as though they actually exist**. When new patterns and new ideas become firmly implanted in your subjective mind, the universe will respond by providing everything you need to make your dreams come true.

... AND THAT'S THE WAY IT REALLY IS!

One of the most dramatic accounts of creating your own future was reported some years ago in all the major newspapers. It was entitled, "Roof-Top Reverend's 14-Million-Dollar Dream Rises."

Of course, the story was about Reverend Robert Schuller and the place was Garden Grove, California. At that point in time, everyone in America, with the exception of one or two people somewhere in the mountains of Virginia, knew of Reverend Schuller.

His dream had become America's dream and people from all over the country were sending him checks, large and small, to complete his dream. How did he accomplish this?

Reverend Schuller painted a picture so vivid in the minds of his listeners that they wanted desperately to share in his dream. He created the desire by describing, in detail, the vision that was in his mind.

His vision was of a magnificent building and inside would stand a pulpit twelve feet high on a crimson marble platform. There would be glass above and all around so that the only thing visible would be the sky. The balconies would seat two thousand people, the main floor another two thousand, and the choir loft would seat five hundred. I think you would agree that most churches in this country today would be happy to have five hundred people in the entire congregation. Yet Reverend Schuller envisioned five hundred people in the choir, before his church was ever built.

CREATIVE IMAGINATION
What You "See" Is What You Get

Reverend Schuller began his ministry in 1955 with his wife as the only member. For want of money, for want of property, for want of a place, he spent six years on the roof top of a snack bar, at a drive-in theater. For six years there was nothing but space between his eyes and the continuous dynamic view of the shifting clouds in the sky.

Isn't it significant that what he saw each day, when he was on the roof top of that drive-in theater, is now what you see when you visit the spectacular Crystal Cathedral?

Is this a coincidence? No! This man is a dreamer. He has great imagination, great conviction, and the enthusiasm to set the dreams of his imagination in motion.

Negative use of the imagination

(What you see is what you get, but not necessarily what you want!)

Of course, in the paragraphs above, we are talking about the creative use of the imaging power. Unfortunately, most people will use their imagination to see repeatedly what they have, in the past, already seen and created. In this way they become "locked in" to what already is.

... AND THAT'S THE WAY IT REALLY IS!

By becoming locked into what already is, they shut themselves out of what could be. When this happens, a person becomes afraid of the unknown while becoming increasingly comfortable with what is. They settle down into an uncomfortable comfort zone and are afraid to emerge.

An example of a person being in a comfort zone is an alcoholic. Surely you would believe every alcoholic would like to get well. For many, this is not true because they are **afraid** to emerge from their unacceptable comfort zone.

Fortunately, through Alcoholics Anonymous, others who have emerged from this fear, can share the image of a life that is superior. They can cause the practicing alcoholic to catch a glimpse of the wonderful things life can offer.

When the alcoholic takes this new vision into his or her own mind, sobriety begins. Not only physical sobriety begins, but a multitude of other delightful, exciting experiences begin to emerge.

There is another type of imagination that is not constructive. If you are escaping from reality, **for long periods of time**, by using your imagination to create imaginary worlds, you are **fantasizing**.

This use of the imagination is not creative. It is destructive. It will paralyze you by making you immobilized. It will rob you of forward motion and prevent you from taking action.

CREATIVE IMAGINATION
What You "See" Is What You Get

To paraphrase, Albert Einstein, "Imagination is more important than knowledge, for knowledge is limited. Imagination embraces the entire world. It stimulates progress and gives birth to the evolution of mankind."

Let me repeat. Your mind is a goal-seeking, goal-achieving mechanism. If you do not give it new goals, if you do not give it new worlds to conquer, it will keep on conquering what it has already conquered. It maintains the status quo and that becomes the most unexciting, unappealing life you could imagine. This is where all disease and stagnation come into your experience.

Creative imagination is evident when you build a dream with your imagination that is so real and vivid, it must come true. It has no choice because the whole universe responds to, and confirms, the visions of your consciousness.

Employing the Imagination

The dictionary defines "imagine" as follows: "To form a mental picture or image of, to create in the mind, or to **employ** the imagination." You can actually put your imagination to **work**. You may "employ" it.

The Latin meaning of imagine is "to picture to one's self," in other words, to picture to yourself, that which you would like to experience. Another way to

... AND THAT'S THE WAY IT REALLY IS!

state it would be to foresee, meaning to see or to know beforehand. To foresee means to know of an occurrence in advance of its coming into existence, or to anticipate it.

Everything that has been created upon this earth by man was created in someone's mind. It was envisioned. They could foresee the can opener, the home, the office building, and even the most complex of electronic gadgetry. Some things in existence, like modern day automobiles, had to be created by many different people. Someone or a group of people envisioned the outer body styling. Other people fashioned the interior design, and others, the mechanical mechanisms. All these things were mental images produced by the imagination. The same mental imaging takes place in the mind of every fulfilled person who has ever lived.

People who live dynamic, expressive, fulfilled lives do not come into that experience by chance. It does not just happen. It can only occur through an understanding of the nature of the mind and its relation to the universe.

The creative use of the imagination involves learning how to cooperate with the super-intelligence from which great artistic achievements, new discoveries, and new ideas spring forth. In this book, we are learning how to deliberately work with the imagination to bring new experiences into being.

CREATIVE IMAGINATION
What You "See" Is What You Get

There is a very important quotation by Rufus Jones. Read it carefully. "Getting your imagination captured is almost the whole of life." I hope you have been "capturing" your imagination by writing down ideas for goals as you have been reading these pages. It is very important to capture even the wildest of imaginings by writing them down immediately. You might think you will remember them and jot them down later, but you will not! Your most important revelation may escape you as a result of this procrastination.

The minute the eyes of your heart are enlightened, the minute your imagination gives you the picture of your path, of your goal — **capture your vision!** It is as good as done!

Capturing Your Imagination

The way to become the architect of your fate and the captain of your soul is to capture your imagination. A remarkable architect once told me how he accomplished the process of creating new structures. He said, "After having seen the property or viewing pictures of it, I approach the property in my imagination. While walking toward it, I ask my mind what kind of building needs to be in this place? What kind of form is appropriate? What is to take place in this structure? Who is to inhabit it? What kinds of persons will be there? What great purpose will be served as a result of its existence?"

... AND THAT'S THE WAY IT REALLY IS!

"As I ask these questions in my mind, the structure that is to be, slowly begins to unfold and grow in my consciousness. As I see it more clearly, I must write it down. I must capture what I see and **what I see**, becomes the drawing of the **structure** that will be."

You are the architect of your life and you must capture these wild birds of fancy that fly through your imagination. You must reach up and pick them off, quickly committing them to paper, so they will begin to form lines that take shape in your thought.

Boss Kettering, the inventive genius who developed the electric starter for automobiles and the first electric cash register, wanted so much to conclusively prove the power of visualization, imagination, and goal-setting, that he made a substantial bet of five thousand dollars with a friend. His bet was, that if his friend would put a beautiful ornate bird cage in the foyer of his house, someday his friend would be forced to put a bird in the bird cage.

Boss Kettering knew his friend would encounter many obstacles. All kinds of people were bound to say strange things about that bird cage. One day his friend would just have to give up and put a bird in it. When he did, it would cost him five thousand dollars. Incidentally, part of the deal was, he could not tell anyone that the presence of the cage was the result of a bet.

CREATIVE IMAGINATION
What You "See" Is What You Get

His friend took the bet and put the ornate bird cage in the foyer of his house. Many parties were held in this home and friends would come by and say, "What a magnificent bird cage! It's the most beautiful bird cage I have ever seen. If I ever have a bird cage I would want one just as wonderful. Where did you ever find it?"

His reply varied, but his favorite was that he and his decorator looked at all the catalogs in a famous furniture mart and picked this bird cage out because it tied in with the decor of the rest of the house. At least it sounded somewhat logical.

Invariably his guest would say: "Where is your bird?" And the conversation would continue something like this: "I don't have a bird." The guest might say, "Did he die?" "No! He didn't die. I don't have a bird and, furthermore, I never intended to get a bird. Everyone is hung-up on something. With me, it just happens to be bird cages!"

So, he kept seeing the bird cage. And he kept watching his guests see what a beautiful bird cage he had ... but he had no bird.

Finally he succumbed. He bought a magnificent bird and put it in the bird cage! It cost him five thousand dollars but he could withstand it no longer.

The point is ... be careful of what kind of bird cages you hang up in your life. If you put a cage there, eventually it will be occupied by a bird.

... AND THAT'S THE WAY IT REALLY IS!

The unoccupied bird cage reminds me of a story told to me by a young woman who had set a goal for the acquisition of a husband. She had created in her mind the kind of person she wanted, carefully listing the traits and qualities she desired. She was explaining to me that she had created a powerful vacuum, one that was sure to provide results. So I asked, "What is this great powerful vacuum?" She replied without hesitation, "I only sleep in half of the bed!"

CHAPTER VII

"THE NITTY GRITTY"

It is now time to take the long list of desires you have written on paper and examine them more thoroughly. You will notice I called them "desires" and not goals.

You will also see that they fall into several categories like **career**, **family**, or **things I want to do**. I know that it is impossible to completely separate career goals from family goals, any more than you can separate physical goals from mental goals. They are all interconnected and interrelated when working with the "whole person" concept. By making your desires and plans come together for each category of your life, you will be developing a plan for revitalizing your whole being.

At this time you have, without regard to importance or significance to your life, merely accumulated a long list of ideas which have passed through your mind. Eventually we will be sorting out these ideas, and keeping only those that have quality enough to become your goals.

... AND THAT'S THE WAY IT REALLY IS!

One reason why some goals are never reached is they are isolated goals, without any connecting or supporting goals. A classic example is most people who decide to lose weight. They establish a weight loss goal, fifteen pounds for instance, and start to work toward their goal. The problem lies in the **lack of excitement** generated by the loss of a few pounds on the way to their goal. Most of the excitement only comes when a person reaches their goal.

A better way is to set up the weight loss as a goal but also include the more exciting goal of a new wardrobe, new friends, new adventures, and a whole new look.

Can you see how goals in entirely different categories support each other? With this in mind let us place your desires into twelve different goal categories.

▼ Career

This first category contains all the desires and dreams connected with your chosen pursuit or your life's work. Establishing levels of accomplishment, advancing your career position and developing the skills needed to be effective are examples.

▼ Financial

This category includes such goals as getting a raise, getting out of debt, building a certain net

"THE NITTY GRITTY"

worth by a specified time or retiring at a pre-established time with a given net worth.

These goals must be realistic. A friend read ***"Think and Grow Rich"*** and set a goal of having fifty-thousand dollars in the bank by the end of one month. In reality he currently was in debt fifteen thousand dollars, and in addition, was unemployed. Is that a realistic goal? Certainly not! First things must come first. My friend's first goal should have been to become employed. His second goal should have been to get out of debt. I am sure the author of ***"Think and Grow Rich,"*** Napoleon Hill, would agree wholeheartedly with the lack of believability in my friend's goals.

Do not set a goal of climbing Pike's Peak while you are down in a diving suit two hundred feet below the level of the ocean. First, come back to sea level and then start climbing from there.

▼ Spiritual

As you will discover, a goal in this category could be to become a part of a Master Mind group. This concept will be explained in detail later. Another goal could be to learn how to practice spiritual principles in all of your affairs.

... AND THAT'S THE WAY IT REALLY IS!

▼ Physical

How we feel physically affects our ability to function mentally, and can affect our sense of self worth. Example goals could be: eating with more selectivity, losing or gaining weight, and ultimately to maintain an ideal weight. Improving our physical appearance, by improving our wardrobe or learning new grooming and make-up procedures, can make a world of difference in how we feel about ourselves. Possibly, we might want to take up exercising, jogging, join a health spa, or even give up smoking.

▼ Mental

We might set a goal of improving our memory for names. We can enhance our creative ability by learning how to tap into the mind's super powers. We can further our education in preparation for a future task in life. We can improve our speaking ability and eliminate erroneous mental attitudes.

▼ Family

Improving relationships with our spouse, parents, or children could be life-changing goals. For example, if you have children over twenty-one years of age who have left home, and you are still grieving over it, you should

"THE NITTY GRITTY"

set a goal to no longer grieve. If you are a child over twenty-one, are still living at home, and your parents are grieving about it, you should set a goal to break the ties that are holding both you and your parents in bondage. Your family goals change with time and you need to be sure they are up to date. Providing better necessities of life for your family, and an education for your children, could be a goal for some. For others, the goal could be to assist in the providing of family necessities, and the education of other family members.

▼ Personal relationships

Setting goals in the area of personal relationships can be one of the most rewarding things you can do for yourself. By establishing the type of relationships you desire, you will attract those individuals who fit the description. Conversely, **you** must remember to always do your best to fit the description that would attract the type of individuals you desire.

One goal in this category could be to become best friends with your spouse. Couples who demonstrate this relationship find happiness far beyond the comprehension of those who have not chosen to have this experience.

... AND THAT'S THE WAY IT REALLY IS!

Sometimes, releasing old relationships can be a very worthwhile goal. Always living in the past keeps us from our good and has the effect of keeping the foul odor of stagnation heavy upon us. We must do whatever is necessary to break away from the crystallization of the past.

▼ Things I Want To Do

Would you like to travel? Take a cruise? Go on a safari? Would you like to write a book? Would you like to go deep sea-fishing? Even catch a sailfish? Are you thinking "Impossible"? I say, "Nonsense!" Write those desires and goals down and watch yourself be amazed at the results!

▼ Things I Want To Be

Maybe you would like to be an accomplished public speaker, maybe even a minister. Would you like to be a singer? If so, set a goal to take voice lessons. Want to learn to play a guitar? Set a goal to have a guitar, then to take lessons, or possibly learn from a friend.

"THE NITTY GRITTY"

▼ Things I Want To Have

This list could be a long one, but write it anyway. Maybe you want a new watch, a dream house, a new car, or a snowblower. Possibly instead of a snowblower, a special someone to shovel the snow might even be better!

Speaking of dream houses, a champion goal-setting friend of mine called one day while I was making notes for an evening class. My secretary told him I was busy preparing a lesson and just could not talk to anyone at that moment, but he insisted. "I have to talk to Jack," he told her. My instructions to my personal secretary have always been that an emergency in the eyes of the beholder is an emergency, so she asked me to take the call.

"Jack, I just have to tell you about my miracle, my goal-setting miracle." I could tell that he was so excited he could hardly stand it and I replied, "Don, do you know that I'm right in the midst of making some notes on my goal-setting class?" He said, "I didn't even know you were doing one."

... AND THAT'S THE WAY IT REALLY IS!

Now, you must know, as background, that in a previous goal-setting class, Don had written down a description of his dream home. It was a very beautiful, expensive, two-story house on a lake, hidden by trees. It had an "old brick" look, and had large windows with many small panes of glass. It had gray-stained wood on the upper story and steep upper roof lines that accented its silhouette, giving it a rustic appearance. Inside, the living room had a cathedral ceiling with a large, stone fireplace. From this room, a panoramic view of the peaceful lake setting could be experienced from his leather easy chair. In his mind, his description of his dream house was clear, and his feelings about it were deep and sincere.

In time, he bought for himself a smaller, but still quite elegant house. The day before he called me, some of his appointments were canceled and his plans for the day were changed. Just at that moment, his Realtor called and said, "I have a special house I want you to see."

Don replied that he had a fine house. "You should know I have a house that meets my needs because you sold it to me." His Realtor said, "This is a special house." Don objected further, that it was not a good time to look at a house and that it would be a waste of time.

"THE NITTY GRITTY"

After some convincing, they went to see the house anyway.

They turned off the road, went down a lane through the tall trees and there it was, exactly as Don had described on paper and captured in his mind. There was his dream home, beautiful, two-stories tall, with ducks on the lake ... the bricks ... the fireplace, and the view. He couldn't believe his eyes, but it was too expensive, of course. "Maybe not," said his Realtor. "The owners need to sell it right now and an immediate sale will get you a bargain price."

Don's mind started to work in a way most of us experience. "I already have a house with no prospective buyers and I doubt if I can get a loan from the bank before selling my present home."

They went straight to the bank and at the price that was being quoted, there was no problem provided Don could come up with an additional $50,000.

Don put his house on the market and within 48 hours it was sold to a couple who just happened to have $50,000 in cash. Do you believe it? I know it! I get reports of this kind of demonstration, constantly.

... AND THAT'S THE WAY IT REALLY IS!

Don remarked, "Anything we dare dream and then implement with enthusiasm and action, will begin to unfold in the most natural and remarkable way."

Don is a dreamer, but more than that. I have never ever in my life caught Don in the "Lotus Position," meaning that he not only dreams his dreams, but he then goes into action. He goes out into his days and his nights doing the things that ought to be done by him, practicing spiritual principles in all of his affairs.

Remember that a vision held in the mind with feeling, becomes a fact, and whatever the mind of man can conceive (whatever your mind can become "pregnant with") and believe, will become your experience.

Believe means to "give permission." It means to "invite into your experience." In French, believe means "to bring to a head."

You will achieve your goals and dreams in an effortless way but the effort will come in the imagining and in the believing. It will come in holding true to a steady course, straight for that which you have chosen.

"THE NITTY GRITTY"

▼ Feelings

There is no substitute for feeling good. This category includes goals that reflect positive attitudes and positive emotional changes, such as experiencing joy each day no matter what is happening. It includes being excited, awake, alert, alive, enthusiastic, and surrendering resentments, irritability, anger, blame, and guilt. The progress you make with your feelings will determine your success in all other goal categories.

▼ Miscellaneous

Whatever doesn't fit into any of the other groups, put it here.

… AND THAT'S THE WAY IT REALLY IS!

Surprise! I have news for *some* of you!

You may be complacently sitting there in your easy chair or relaxing in your bed, thinking you have "put one over" on this experienced teacher, but I have news for you. Experience and an understanding of human behavior teaches me that there are one, two, or **more** of you, that have not yet written down even one goal!

I congratulate those of you who have written some of your goals, and I implore those of you who have not, to forgive yourselves. It's OK. In fact it's almost normal. One of our problems is that we mentally beat up on ourselves when we have not accomplished all that we have desired. Old patterns are hard to break. **BUT!**

NOW is the time to change. For those of you in this predicament, get up and find a pen and pad. Start by writing just **one** desire or goal. Place it in its appropriate category and feel the sense of accomplishment this positive action brings forth. This small act will open the door to your success. By going into action and breaking inertia, you have set a standard that is repeatable. It is repeatable with much greater ease, each successive time you choose to accomplish it.

All progress, whether individual or collective, is because someone dared to perceive a mental image never before seen in reality. You have now dared to be successful. If you support your vision with deep feeling, your desires will be fulfilled.

"THE NITTY GRITTY"

Those of you who had previously written your desires, and those of you who have just taken the giant step of writing your first desire, must decide which of your desires you would have as actual living experiences. Remember that no one but you can decide for you, and no one can dream for you. God can inspire you, but the choice is always yours.

Take your dreams and put them together in the twelve natural categories or compartments I have outlined for you. Your goal is to be a whole person, so believe and feel as you are categorizing your goals that you are putting your life together. Remind yourself that whatever the mind of man can conceive and believe, it will experience. Your subconscious mind does not know the difference between your imaginings and that which is real.

Don's subconscious mind took his dream as reality and created the equivalent in the home that is now his to enjoy. Give yourself permission to move into these experiences.

A friend discussed with me his dream of being an artist. I asked him if he had any talent and he said he did. He said, "It's raw talent." I asked, "Why don't you take your raw talent and let someone who can instruct you bring it into a creative flare?"

... AND THAT'S THE WAY IT REALLY IS!

The world is full of educated derelicts and of people who have raw talent, but raw talent will not do it, it really will not. So, my friend found a teacher, an artist of great ability, a person of some renown in that part of the country. This teacher was recognized for many artistic accomplishments, but his primary claim to fame was national recognition for his painting of a cow! Can you imagine someone achieving national recognition for painting a cow? Ah, but this was an unusual cow. The painting was so perfect that it was reproduced on the cover of a cattlemen's magazine, and the farmers who saw it were astonished when they saw this picture of the perfect cow.

They had never seen a perfect cow, and were amazed that a perfect cow existed. But wait a minute. It must exist, because there was its picture.

I asked my friend, "How did your teacher come to paint a perfect cow?" He explained that his teacher went to the cattlemen's association in Kansas City, and found out what elements were most desirable in the ideal cow. Then he found pictures of different cattle possessing these desirable traits ... the hind quarters of one ... the tail of another ... the head of another, and he put them together into a composite photograph.

When he had put all these pieces together, he painted what he saw, reproducing in visual form what the world had never seen before, the only perfect cow.

"THE NITTY GRITTY"

Maybe your wish is not to paint the perfect cow, but you can certainly create in your imagination a more nearly perfect life than the one that you have yet demonstrated. Is that not true?

In fact, you have already started. The brush strokes are already there. The lines and the shape have begun to take form. A portrait of life, so exciting it is still beyond your imagination, is on the canvas, and is becoming vivid with color. Its message to the universe is rapidly approaching the clarity of pure crystal.

Now, in the same way that the artist formed the perfect cow, put all of your desires and goals into a composite structure. Examine each of these categories, and arrange them in a manner that will cause your life to unfold in a perfect way. In this process, a whole new experience begins to take form and shape.

The author, Clarence Buttington Klein, stated in one of his books that he believed he discovered the one great moving, compelling force which makes every man what he becomes in the end. That force, was not love. It was not religion, virtue or ambition. It was your **imagination**.

CHAPTER VIII

THE IMAGE BOOK

A Visual Roadmap for the Subconscious

Albert Einstein was once asked what he would like most to say to the science students in America's schools. Without hesitation, he replied, "I would ask them to spend an hour every day rejecting the ideas of others, and thinking things out for themselves."

I am sure that Dr. Einstein was not saying we should ignore the opinions of other people. Have you noticed how we tend to let conditions, peer groups, or parents determine what we think and what we believe?

A great deal of what we think is not really what **we** think at all. It has been programmed into our minds by our experiences. We fail to think for ourselves.

In the same manner that we fail to think for ourselves in our belief systems, we fail to think in deciding what we want from life. We submissively accept whatever comes our way and we wonder why we are unhappy with the results.

... AND THAT'S THE WAY IT REALLY IS!

If you were to ask the next one hundred people you meet, "What do you want most in life?" Ninety-eight percent of them would not be able to tell you. If you persist and press them for an answer, some of them will say security. Others will say money, others happiness, others fame and power, others social recognition, others ease in living; and the list continues.

One person might say, "I want to be a singer. Even though I do not have much of a voice, I want to be a singer," or, "I would like to write a book, or I would like to become a minister." We are always looking for an easier, softer way, and obviously being a minister is the easier, softer way. Nothing could be easier than that! Maybe this person would like to be married. That might even be easier than becoming a minister!

None of these people will be able to define the terms to you, or give you the slightest indication of a plan by which they hope to obtain these vaguely expressed wishes. In reality, they have not given it much thought. They hope their good will come to them, but wishing will not make it so. Prosperity, goal-achieving, and balanced lives do not respond to wishes. They respond only to definite plans, backed by intense definite desires, that continue through consistent persistence.

Remember that goal-achieving is a science and that the dreams and desires of your heart will not happen by chance. In this universe, there is no "chance." We are in a divinely ordered universe that works by laws. As one

THE IMAGE BOOK
A Visual Roadmap for the Subconscious

of this universe's expressions, you must understand and practice these laws to experience what your heart desires.

Do you have a chief aim in life? What do you wish to do with the rest of your life? Only you can decide. There is no one else qualified to make these decisions.

Somewhere along the way you must come up with solid answers, and then you must convince your mind that this is what you are going to do. Not what you **hope** might happen, but what you are going to **do**. Before a goal can be achieved, your mind must come to see it clearly, believe in it, feel it, and hold it dear.

In a recent goal-achieving class, a young woman had listed over two hundred desires by the end of the first week. By the second week, the count was approaching three hundred. She had placed them in their appropriate categories and in addition, had arranged them in order of importance within each category.

This young woman was not hesitant to ask of life what she desired. Just four weeks earlier, she won a car in a raffle. Remarkably, just two weeks before the raffle, she was very frustrated in her mind. Her frustration was over not being able to decide whether she was going to keep the car or take the money! Do you see why she won the raffle? In fact, she was present at the drawing. She told her friend who was seated beside her, "Give me plenty of room because when they draw my number, I'm going to jump and squeal." So they drew her number and she jumped and squealed.

... AND THAT'S THE WAY IT REALLY IS!

She had a desire and saw it clearly. One way to convince the mind and give it clear vision is to use the principle of the "Image Book." This young woman just recently spent fourteen hours creating an image book that has become the equivalent of her new goals.

Our outer world and all that it contains is but the visible duplicate of our inner mind state. If we wish to change our life experience, then we must change our mind. We must change our thinking and our feeling.

My self image determines my life experience. My experience is on a moment-to-moment basis and can be no higher and no lower than the invisible image of life I have in my mind. What I see myself doing in my mind is what I will ultimately end up doing in my life ... no more, no less.

You are setting the perimeters of your life by the images that come naturally to your mind. When you make an image book, you cut out words and pictures that are descriptive of the real you, this perfect self of you that is now reforming and reshaping your destiny. You then place these words and pictures in the pages of a photo album or a note book, and arrange them to describe how you would like your life to be.

You may not immediately feel the images you have created, and you may not believe in them at the moment, but they describe how you intend to feel. You will be working with these images until you come to believe that this artistic creation is actually your life.

THE IMAGE BOOK
A Visual Roadmap for the Subconscious

You are the architect of your life and this is your new plan. You can create one or several pages on various aspects of your life that you wish to have changed or expanded.

These pages do not have to be extremely artistic or complex to be effective, however, some of you will take great pleasure in creating pages of beauty.

Simplicity sometimes is even **better** than complexity. A successful businessman wanted to increase order in his personal and business affairs. He created one page in his image book that simply stated, "I ENJOY ORDER TODAY!" There was nothing else on the page. These four words were life changing to him because they had deep meaning. To someone else, they may be meaningless.

You may create pages that address some of the specific desires or goals you have placed in your categories.

You can create pages on aspects of your life that you want developed or expanded. Make pages that describe your inner qualities such as your femininity or your masculinity, your self-confidence, or your spiritual awareness.

You can create pages describing the outer visible part of your life, such as your surroundings, where you live and how you live, your physical appearance, clothes, cars, and things.

... AND THAT'S THE WAY IT REALLY IS!

In setting your goals and making your image book pages, you should stretch beyond the point of your believability, but do not go beyond the point of possibility.

There are eight principles to follow when making your image book pages:

1. Make your pages personal.

Use your name in your affirmations. Use the words "I am" as in the statement, "I am a renowned speaker who is in great demand." Platitudes like "enthusiasm makes sales" may be true, but have no effect on reconditioning attitudes. More effective words would be "My enthusiasm increases my sales."

2. Keep your goals positive.

Use statements and conditions that you want to exist, rather than statements about things or conditions that you wish to eliminate. Instead of "I do not lose my temper" make it, "I have a beautiful disposition and I am inwardly calm and outwardly poised."

3. Stay in the present tense.

For instance, if you want to take a trip to Hawaii, show yourself as already there. Use pictures and statements that will make you feel the balmy breezes, feel the salty air, and hear the sound of the pounding surf. Affirmations like "I **am going** to be more patient," do not

THE IMAGE BOOK
A Visual Roadmap for the Subconscious

describe a "now" moment. They place your improvement in the some day category. "I am a very patient person" puts the same idea in the now moment.

Normally, our thinking is in the third dimension, in the dimension of weight, height, thickness, time, and space. Our human mind, with its limited reasoning faculties, is stifled by these third dimension boundaries.

Obviously, we must go beyond the land of reason into the world of realization. When the word is broken down, it becomes "real–I–zation." The real "I," the real self of you must take your dreams and cause them to become real. The word realization means to real–ize, to cause something that has not happened yet to become so real that it must happen.

Have you noticed that we do this with our fears? We have had many instructions to fear not. Do not be afraid. In reality, the things that we fear most often come to pass. Why are fears so easy to real–ize?

If you fear a thing, your imagination takes over and your fear becomes very real for you. You anticipate through worry, the occurrence of the thing that you have feared, and in time it will happen. That which I greatly fear has become my experience. This is the **negative** way of using the creative power of your mind.

True real–I–zation requires the doing away of time and space and all conditions. Your spirit is not subject to time and space and therefore, in the now moment, you can go into your mind. You can visualize and feel that your wishes, your desires, your dreams have already come to pass, and this will immediately place you in the fourth dimension. Your dreams are already a reality.

The fourth dimension is timeless. Do you understand why goals should be thought of as already accomplished? There is no need to state that you will accomplish a goal by January 1, because that is a date in time. In the fourth dimension, it is already done — **now**. It will materialize as you walk along the road of life, but in reality it has already occurred.

4 **Have your pages reflect achievement as already achieved.**

Example: "I have a sincere outgoing regard for others" rather than "I am steadily improving my warmth toward others." Eliminate any feelings of anxiety. Anxiety is a message to your subconscious that your dreams have not yet been accomplished.

THE IMAGE BOOK
A Visual Roadmap for the Subconscious

5 **Use your image book pages to change yourself and not others.**

For instance, avoid statements like, "My son respects me." A better wording would be "I am an effective parent and understand my son's point of view."

6 **Avoid comparing yourself with others in your image book pages.**

Instead of the thought "I am the most productive salesperson in this group," you will find it better to state "I am an excellent salesperson and my production is high."

Have your thoughts describe an activity rather than an ability. Give them action. Words such as "I can be understanding" can be better stated as "I easily understand other people's point of view."

Maintain accuracy and balance. Remember, growth is taken one step at a time. Be realistic. If you are $5,000 in debt, affirm that "I am completely solvent and love the feeling of successfully running my financial life" rather than "I am independently wealthy and free to do whatever I choose." Your goals should be designed to help you grow. They must encourage you to stretch and break out of your comfort zone.

... AND THAT'S THE WAY IT REALLY IS!

7 **Maintain positive excited feelings.**

Goals and affirmations are powerless unless you accompany them with good feelings. For example, "I weigh one hundred and sixty-five pounds and feel wonderful" is more alive than simply saying "I weigh one hundred and sixty-five pounds." "I am proud of the fact that I am a good public speaker" has more impact on your feeling nature than simply saying, "I am a good public speaker."

You describe yourself as you want to be through the pictures and words that you place on each page. Then you work with those pages every day and really feel them. You visualize them and you keep persisting until your mind finally begins to accept them as real.

The purpose of these daily exercises is to call forth the qualities that already exist in you. As you do this, remember that this energy, this "ether," in which we live, in which we move, and in which we have our being, is entrapping these mind pictures in a positive way. This positive entrapment produces not a photograph but a living experience.

After my last goal-achieving class, a young man who has been working with these ideas for some time came up to me and said, "Jack, I have been working with these things until my

THE IMAGE BOOK
A Visual Roadmap for the Subconscious

mind hurts. Why have I not been making my demonstration?"

Can you guess why he has not? Some of you have been working on these principles until your mind hurts. Am I right? Carl Young, the eminent psychologist, psychiatrist, knew why.

He said Spirit is something higher than intellect — it includes not only the intellect, but feelings, as well. You are a spiritual being and those feelings that you have must come forth and must take part, must participate, must wrap themselves around your picture.

The ideas and pictures will give birth and will send forth into the visible world, a newly formed entity called your new experience.

I asked my friend if he had done an image book and he said that he had, and furthermore, he went through it and read it often. I said to him, "You must not only read it, you must **feel** it, you must live it, you must **love** it and get so excited about it that it becomes real. You must walk into the images that you create and smell the flowers, feel the grass, touch the rain, and allow the warm breeze to caress your cheek. If a new car is there, you must open the door and smell the leather. You must get behind the wheel, start the engine, feel the power of the engine, slam the door, and drive away."

... AND THAT'S THE WAY IT REALLY IS!

He asked, "Can I do that?" I replied, "Of course you can! In your mind, you can do anything that your heart desires. By working daily with your image book, you can feel the pages come alive as though they have already happened to you. Your five physical senses can only report what has already happened in your life. They are restricted to contact with the world outside yourself. On the other hand, your spiritual sense, your higher sense, your creative imagination, was designed to help you see things that have not yet occurred."

8 **Your obligation to the law is to work with the "feeling" of belief as though your goals were already accomplished.**

Belief is the energy source that carries you to your goals. It is the fuel for the engine of accomplishment. Feelings and belief connect you to the master source that will accomplish your goals effortlessly.

CHAPTER IX

THE LAW OF SECOND FORCE

For every action there is an equal and opposite reaction

Have you wondered why more people do not achieve their goals? Have you wondered why they stop short of success and turn back unfulfilled? There is a natural law, a natural phenomenon that occurs in the third dimension of normal life, that prevents people from realizing accomplishment as their experience.

This is the law of "second force." "First force" is the force of initiation of effort. Every time you move forward or take action toward a goal, you are initiating "first force." Have you noticed how every time you plan to do a thing, there is something that comes out of nowhere to stop your progress? This is the law of "second force" in action.

"Second force" is a phenomenon that you can observe as a neutralizing, nullifying or cancellation of the energy you expend. In the world of physics, this law is stated in the following manner: For every action, there is an equal and opposite reaction. I am sure you are familiar with it.

... AND THAT'S THE WAY IT REALLY IS!

The same law works in the mind. Are not all manifested things, all physical things, mind things first? This is a mind law, not a physics law at all. It is how "second force" works to neutralize your goal-achieving efforts.

I can give you an example: "Jones," said the battled office manager, "How did you do it? You've only been working here two weeks and you're already a month behind." You understand this principle, do you not?

"Second force" is not a force that hits you over the head. It is a force that makes you forget in mid-morning what you have intended to do late tonight. It is a force that starts out with great enthusiasm at first, and then reaches the opposite cycle, which is depression. After being hit with it, you say to yourself, "I wonder how I could have been so optimistic."

Second force can be a type of inertia. Inertia means the tendency of a body to resist acceleration. The Latin form of the word means "idle." It is non-movement. It is non-motion. You know what you should do, but you resist doing it.

An example is one who has a desire and a goal to lose weight. To prove it in your mind, decide right now, whatever your weight is, that you are going to lose ten pounds. Watch what happens in your mind. All kinds of things immediately come to mind that will tell you how difficult the task is. You will think how

THE LAW OF SECOND FORCE
For every action there is an equal and opposite reaction

impossible it is, and besides that, your mind will say, "It really is not necessary!"

Second force can only stop us if we do not have a focused willpower. Our willpower has become an "I cannot power," an "I wonder if I can power," or a "I hope I can power." Here and now, your willpower must become your "I can power."

Just yesterday a young man was sharing with me an example of second force. He told me that not long ago he had an opportunity. It was the greatest opportunity of his life. It came suddenly in a conversation. His dream was there before him. All he had to do was to say yes.

But immediately in his mind, as quick as a flash, came this series of alibis and excuses. He heard himself denying this opportunity. He went on to explain very carefully why it would not be possible for him to take advantage at this time. As he talked to himself, he knew that every word was an absolute lie. He later reflected, "I was saying it because of my fear of criticism. What would people think of me if I would attempt to do this thing, and fail?"

Can you see how second force works in your mind, to cause you to not move forward into the land of your dreams? It's always there. It is natural in the three dimensional world, and **if you do not see it, you will not make your demonstration.**

... AND THAT'S THE WAY IT REALLY IS!

The "third force" is a higher power. It is the force that mankind has recognized since the beginning of time, but has chosen to call it by many different names. No matter what the terminology, there is only one supreme power, one ruler of the universe, and many of us choose to call it, God.

There is a higher power that can neutralize second force, and will, but this neutralizing force does not respond unless, and until, you and I do our part. Second force will always stop us unless we make a decision to take one very important step. Would you like to know this secret that will guarantee success ... the secret that will change your life?

You must persist! Nothing from this moment forward will ever stop you from achieving your goals, if you persist. This must be a conscious, now-moment choice. Your mind must make the choice and your feelings must agree.

CHAPTER X

PERSISTENCE

The word persist means to be obstinately repetitious, to be insistent or tenacious in some activity. It means to hold firmly and steadfastly to some purpose, despite obstacles or setbacks.

I love the word persistence because it absolutely has changed my life. In my first image book, I included this statement called the Legend of Persistence by Calvin Coolidge.

> "Nothing in the world can take the place of persistence. Talent will not. **Genius** will not, education alone will not. Persistence and determination alone are omnipotent."

Persistence and determination are indeed omnipotent, and persistence is ready to color your world with happiness, but you must believe in it fully. On the face of this earth there are less than five percent of the human population who know anything at all about persistence.

... AND THAT'S THE WAY IT REALLY IS!

Persistence does not come as an inherited experience from your parents, and you do not learn it from them. You usually learn persistence from adversity, but adversity need not be a prerequisite to persistence.

Persistence is an essential factor in the procedure of transmuting your visions and your desires into goals achieved. You will never experience them unless you create the powerful determination to succeed, and this determination **must become a feeling**. This important fact is often overlooked. Persistence is not an intellectual thing. It is something that happens in your feeling nature.

Will and power, properly combined, become irresistible, and become the basis of persistence. Lack of persistence is the major cause of failure. You are **sure** to fail if you do not persist. Second force is absolutely guaranteed to wipe you out if you do not persist. It will do so in such a nice and polite way that you will cause yourself and others to believe you tried everything in your power to succeed. You will hear yourself saying, "What's the use of trying? The outcome is inevitable. That's just the way life is." Lack of persistence is a major weakness in the majority of the human race.

Persistence is insurance against failure. Life lets no person on this earth achieve great goals without passing the persistence test. You will be caused to "be stopped in your tracks" within your mind. Your dreams will seem to fall apart. Things will come to pass that will absolutely amaze you in their ability to get in the way ... to stand in the way as road blocks beyond which you cannot pass. If you take them personally, if you react with anger, or with resentment, or with disappointment, you have lost the game.

Persistence can be motivated by four necessary steps:

The first is a **definite purpose backed by a burning desire**.

The second is a **definite plan expressed by going into action**.

The third is **a mind closed tightly against all negative and discouraging influences**. This includes the negative suggestions of friends, relatives and acquaintances. You will no longer be party to the losers.

The fourth is to form **a friendly alliance with one or more persons**. This alliance may be called a Master Mind group and will be discussed in greater detail in a following chapter. In this alliance, members mutually encourage each other to follow through with plans and purpose.

... AND THAT'S THE WAY IT REALLY IS!

Long before I read **"The Greatest Salesman In The World,"** I had caused my mind to believe the words contained in the scroll marked III, about persistence. Og Mandino, the author, expressed these very powerful words so magnificently, that I would like to share them with you now. These are some of the most powerful statements my mind has ever experienced, and I ask you to join me in the total feeling of this commitment. Let your mind speak these words with the conviction of every fiber of your being. This is the way that I feel about the fulfillment of my life.

"If I persist,
if I continue to try,
if I continue to charge forward,"
"I will succeed."
*"I will persist **until** I succeed."*

> *"I was not delivered into this world in defeat, nor does failure course in my veins. I am not a sheep waiting to be prodded by my shepherd. I am a lion and I refuse to talk, to walk, to sleep with the sheep. I will hear not those who weep and complain, for their disease is contagious. Let them join the sheep. The slaughterhouse of failure is not my destiny."*

"I will persist until I succeed."

> *"The prizes of life are at the end of each journey, not near the beginning; and it is not given to me to know how many steps are necessary in*

PERSISTENCE

> *order to reach my goal. Failure I may still encounter at the thousandth step, yet success hides behind the next bend in the road. Never will I know how close it lies unless I turn the corner. Always will I take another step. If that is of no avail, I will take another, and yet another. In truth, one step at a time is not too difficult."*

"I will persist until I succeed."

> *"I will never consider defeat and I will remove from my vocabulary such words and phrases as quit, cannot, unable, impossible, out of the question, improbable, failure, unworkable, hopeless, and retreat; for they are the words of fools. I will avoid despair but if this disease of the mind should infect me then I will work on in despair. I will toil and I will endure. I will ignore the obstacles at my feet and keep mine eyes on the goals above my head, for I know that where dry desert ends, green grass grows."*

"I will persist until I succeed."

> *"I will try, and try, and try again. Each obstacle I will consider as a mere detour to my goal and a challenge to my profession. I will persist and develop my skills as the mariner develops his, by learning to ride out the wrath of each storm."*

... AND THAT'S THE WAY IT REALLY IS!

"I will persist until I succeed."

> *"Henceforth, I will learn and apply another secret of those who excel. Never will I allow any day to end with a failure. Thus will I plant the seed of tomorrow's success."*

"I will persist until I succeed."

> *"Nor will I allow yesterday's success to lull me into today's complacency, for this is the great foundation of failure. I will forget the happenings of the day that is gone, whether they were good or bad, and greet the new sun with confidence that this will be the best day of my life."*

> *"So long as there is breath in me, that long will I persist. For now I know one of the greatest principles of success; if I persist long enough I will win. I will persist and I will win."*

Nothing on earth can defeat me ...
 and that's the way it really is!

CHAPTER XI

CULLING THE FISH

Weeding the Garden of Desires

The universe is trying to give you your "good." Now, are you ready to receive that good? There has to be eagerness on the part of the recipient. Have you been following through and increasing your list of desires? Have you ever tried to give something away to someone who did not want it? It is very difficult and not very exciting. Your secret desires will no longer be secret to the universe if you will put a pen in your hand and give your mind permission to fulfill itself.

Are you now beginning the process of organizing your goals in ways that fit naturally into your mind? Have your isolated goals formed marriages, here and there, to take you forward into new experiences and to a total new state of being?

Being comes before doing or having. I must become this thing that I am so I can do the things that ought to be done by me. In the process of becoming, I must demonstrate those outer things and experiences that become my right ... that become my right by virtue of this newly awakened consciousness.

... AND THAT'S THE WAY IT REALLY IS!

In the Bible, ideas are called fish. When the disciples were fishing and caught fish, it meant they were inspired. When they were not catching fish, it meant they were not inspired, and the master teacher told them to go out a little farther and drop their nets a little deeper. In other words, to go to the place inside themselves where the fish were, where the ideas were.

In writing your list of desires, you have caught some fish. Some of your fish are good sized fish and you have dragged in some fish that made you think, "Gosh, that one is too big for me to handle, I think I'll throw it back." I expect you have caught some unusual fish you did not expect, and that is great. If you have not shocked yourself with the goals you are setting, then you really are not setting your goals very well. You need to create a shocking experience so you can break free from your comfort zones and from the self-imposed limitations that have kept you in a static state.

I bet you have caught some fish you did not know were in the lake. Any good fisherman knows you cannot keep all of your fish. I have suggested to you that you cast your nets out indiscriminately and pull in all the fish, but some of them you are going to have to throw away. There are a few carp in there and maybe some gold fish. There are some ideas that are not worthy of you, and there are some immature fish not big enough to keep. Some of your fish are not even edible, so I would

CULLING THE FISH
Weeding the Garden of Desires

ask you to consider your fish and throw out the obviously bad ones. Do not hesitate to rid yourself of these poor ideas, because as soon as you do, the vacuum created will cause new ideas to form. You will catch some new fish that may be of trophy size.

Maybe you are not a fisherman. Let's consider this in another light. I have asked you to prepare the soil of your mind, and then to plant in that soil, a new garden, a new crop, new seeds, that will produce a series of exciting new experiences.

If you will talk to any successful gardener, he will tell you that you must always be prepared to do some weeding. Besides the weeds, there simply is not enough room for every seed to grow in the area that has been assigned to it, and you will have to remove some of those seeds.

Some of your seeds are weed seeds, and the weed seeds will always have a tendency to absorb the energy and nutrients that should go to the good plants. It would be virtually impossible for you to make the long list of experiences you would desire to be yours, and not plant some weeds in that process,.

At the time you were making the list, weeds were OK. If you will remember, I suggested you write down all the ideas that came to you, but now is the time for pruning.

... AND THAT'S THE WAY IT REALLY IS!

For example, one lady in a recent goal-setting class came to me and said, "In looking over my list, I discovered that too many of my goals had to do with traveling. I wanted to go to Europe and South America, Africa and Australia, to the East coast and to the West coast and down South and up North. I discovered that what I really wanted to do was to escape from where I was, to escape from the dullness of my life."

Do you get the point? Some of your goals are significant perhaps, but not very important in establishing the overall framework of a pattern for your life. Be perfectly willing and even eager to take out some of these counter-productive goals. Put on your gardener's gloves and weed your garden of ideas.

CHAPTER XII

INVENTORY

A Searching and Fearless Look at Ourselves

It is now time to consider another list. Napoleon Hill said that no man has a chance to enjoy permanent success until he begins to look in the mirror for the real cause of his mistakes. I must be able to see that the only person who has ever "done me in," is me.

You cannot become a power in your area of responsibility, you cannot achieve any worthwhile undertaking, nor can you permanently demonstrate any of your goals until you have become big enough to accept personal responsibility for your mistakes. More than that, you must be willing to take a sharp look at yourself and see if anything is going to stand between you and these new goals.

For example, suppose that on your list is the goal of acquiring a new position. You enjoy your work and you have done it well, but you have been there for a long time and now feel as if you should be moving on to greater heights.

... AND THAT'S THE WAY IT REALLY IS!

Stand outside yourself for a moment and look at yourself. See if you would hire you! If you would not, why not? Would you want you to work for you? You must become the equivalent of that which you expect. If you can immediately begin to see some flaws which exist, some chinks in your armor, write them down. I can make you this promise. What you see, other people will also see. In fact, they will see it more quickly.

If by chance, one of your goals is to demonstrate a meaningful relationship with a member of the opposite sex, leading to the ceremony of matrimony, take a searching and fearless look at yourself. If you were the other person, would you marry you? If you would not, why not?

You will not be able to get anywhere until you become big enough to accept personal responsibility. If you are not sure, go to your Master Mind group, or persons of like mind, and ask them if they will tell you. I guarantee, they will tell you.

James Cooper said, "He who lacks imagination lives with half a life. He has his experience, he has his facts, he has his learning, but do any of these really live unless touched by the magic of imagination?" So long as the road is straight, man can see down it and follow it, but imagination loops around the turns and gazes far off into the distance. Imagination walks hand in hand with vision.

INVENTORY
A Searching and Fearless Look at Ourselves

Your imagination is important, but it cannot fulfill your heart's desires unless you follow the rules. You must take those steps that will allow you to see yourself clearly. A part of your imagination is not only to set your goals, but also to see the things that are going to keep you from demonstrating those goals. You must work to correct the defects and shortcomings that stand in your way. You must become the equivalent of the experiences you seek.

Inertia

Embracing inertia is one of our faults that is often subtle, yet, it has a profound effect on our happiness. Of course, its presence makes the realization of our goals an impossibility.

One of the great paradoxes of our human nature is that inertia is the driving force in many, if not most, of our basic decisions. Our unwillingness to make a move, moves us more than any other factor. It is startling that we, as spiritual beings, spend great periods of time on earth locked into old forms and shapes, with inertia being our dominant force.

We are beings that were destined to know great movement or motion. Our energy was meant to be transformed into experiences. If you have not yet chosen to use the energy of life, and the energy of the universe, to reform and reshape your world, you are in a state of stagnation.

... AND THAT'S THE WAY IT REALLY IS!

A person who is not in motion is a non-goal person and will, in time, become a crisis creator. If you are a person who does not believe in achieving goals you must, in that non-belief of goals, create the excitement and the fulfillment that your heart intuitively desires, by creating crisis after crisis. Becoming aware of this principle could be a very "eye opening" experience.

The word, "crisis," means, by definition, a crucial point or situation in the course of doing anything. Crisis is from the Greek word meaning "turning point," or a point in the story or drama at which hostile forces are in the most tense state of opposition. If we are not moving forward into new experiences, we are in opposition to ourselves. If we are in opposition to ourselves, that opposition, in time, becomes a crisis or a turning point.

Your life is a story. It is a drama that is unfolding and your self-created crises can be those problems that have most recently afflicted you. They may even be those problems that have caused you to seek knowledge and self improvement.

The wonderful news is, these problems and this crisis can be the most important turning points you have ever experienced in your life. They can be the catalyst that gets you back on track and starts you moving forward again into exciting new experiences.

Not "living your own life" is a trap many people today have fallen into, in the most subtle way. People have allowed their excitement to come from outside

INVENTORY
A Searching and Fearless Look at Ourselves

themselves, through things like soap operas, movies, novels, watching sporting events, television, and hundreds of similar non-participation events.

Now, do not hear me say that watching these non-participation activities is totally bad. It is the **total immersion** in these things and events that is stifling to our spirit.

When we have settled down into the stagnation that comes from non-movement, not having goals and not moving forward, that stagnation causes us to realize we do not have a life of our own. Our spirit causes us to seek excitement by living someone else's life, as in a novel or a soap opera.

I received a letter from a couple who had discovered their goals were not progressing as well as they desired. They decided to look, but even more than that, to search for their stumbling blocks.

"We realized we wanted more out of life, and we saw we were spending too much time just watching television. We made a firm decision. We covered the television with a piece of cloth and then wrote on the cloth with big bold letters, 'We will make our **own** dreams.' Since making this firm decision, we have been working much harder to create our dreams. We have been creating new pictures and new goals. It is absolutely amazing how rapidly our lives are changing for the better."

... AND THAT'S THE WAY IT REALLY IS!

If **you** do not create your own images, your mind will automatically pick up on forms and shapes that are not your own. It will try its best to have those images be its own. This then becomes a non-life, because it is not **from** you and **of** you.

Inertia is a diseased state of the mind. We must diligently, and with frequency, take a fearless and searching inventory of our lives to ascertain that we are moving ahead. If we discover we are in stagnation, we must make a conscious and definite decision to go into action.

The *slightest action* **totally destroys inertia**. It becomes easy to accelerate, and the joy that comes as we increase our forward progress is almost indescribable.

CHAPTER XIII

DEVELOP AND "HONOR" A FLEXIBLE PLAN

Now that you have established some important goals for your life, it is time to develop a plan. Better yet, we should say plans, in the plural, for the accomplishment of these important goals.

If you set a goal that is important enough to be your experience, that goal should be given the honor of a plan, a plan to bring it to reality. You should honor your goal by considering it, by thinking about it, and by loving it. You should work with that specific goal and establish its own personal plan.

For example, suppose you have had a dream for many years to move into a newer, nicer neighborhood and into a larger, lovelier dwelling. Make a plan! Think about all the details. Let that wonderful mind of yours go to work.

What are the first things that are to be done by you to accomplish your goal? Write them down, and after you have written down what you think is the first order of things, write down what will be involved next. Plan it just as you would plan a military operation.

... AND THAT'S THE WAY IT REALLY IS!

Remember, plans are not perfect, nor are they ever complete. They can always be changed.

In fact, plans **should** be changed as they unfold. A General, in time of war, would change his plans to meet with the changing conditions of battle, would he not?

Your life may not be a battlefield, although at times it may seem that way, but be prepared to "hang loose" with your plans and to let them be reformed and reshaped.

Would you like to be a happy homemaker? Then make a plan.

Would you like to reorganize your office or become more effective in your work? Make a plan. Then, make yourself **follow the plan**!

Frank Richardson was a salaried employee working for a small company. He had nothing against his job and it paid good money, but he was always broke. He knew that he would never earn a great deal of money working for that company. It was a comfortable job, but even the president did not make all that much money.

Along with blaming the high cost of living, Frank blamed a great deal of his money problems on his wife's mismanagement of her personal affairs. He had many excuses for how things were. In thinking about your life, you understand Frank Richardson, do you not?

DEVELOP AND "HONOR" A FLEXIBLE PLAN

After all, he made more money than many of his other friends and acquaintances. His job was too good to quit, but not good enough to keep, and so he just kept drifting along. Deeper than money, he felt unfulfilled and uncompleted, until one day he picked up a magazine, a **"Reader's Digest."**

He opened it to a page and there was a sentence that changed his life. It read, "No successful house was ever built, no successful sale was ever made, no successful life was ever lived, without a plan."

Frank thought, "What if I had a plan? What if I could determine, in advance, what my days would be like?" Then, second force sneaked in with its ugly head. "All I do is go to work. I know what I am going to do all day long. I do it and then I come home. My life is so simple, I don't need a plan."

The idea would not let him go. After a week or two of thinking about it, he decided to plan what he would do on his next weekend. Furthermore, he wrote it out in detail.

He selected a time to awake in the morning and began to think about the things he had to do. It occurred to him that it would be a good idea to get the important things out of the way first. He let his imagination begin to run loose, designing the perfect order of events. His Saturday was so inspiring that he began to plan his perfect Sunday.

... AND THAT'S THE WAY IT REALLY IS!

Then, a remarkable thing happened. He found himself looking forward to that weekend all during the week. It had been many years since he had looked forward to a weekend, and his excitement was like a miracle.

At times, he thought it would be difficult to stick to his plan, but he forgot one of the basic laws of mind action. When you send a plan to the subconscious mind and ask the subconscious mind to cooperate with you in shaping something, the subconscious mind goes into action. It helps you carry out the plan, the same plan that it also helped you to form. It executes the plan for you.

The end product was the most interesting and productive weekend of Frank's life. It was so good that he began planning his work days as well as his free time. He actually started planning everything. If he had a free fifteen minutes, he would plan it.

Incidentally, he never felt chained to his plans. If something unexpected came up, he rolled with the punch and remained flexible. Somewhere he had learned a very important principle about non-resistance.

Frank decided he would not resist interruptions or unexpected developments, but instead would make a friend of all these things. If something seemed to get in the way, he would not react with anger, but would smile and compliment the thing that was getting in his way.

DEVELOP AND "HONOR" A FLEXIBLE PLAN

Frank became a changed person. Because he was a changed person, his attitude necessarily also changed, and before long, an opportunity for another job came along.

This happened in a very natural way, but the job was a very challenging job, calling for far more talent and ability than Frank had ever seemed to demonstrate. He was afraid and apprehensive, but knew that if he took the job, if all went well, he would earn more money than he had ever earned before. His family would have freedoms never before experienced.

With great apprehension, he decided to take a chance and accept the new position. He took six months leave of absence just to be sure (why not, if his present employer agreed), but never had to go back to his old job. Within a short time Frank was earning more money than the president of his previous place of employment.

The important thing was not that Frank took another job. It was that he took with him a plan. He had developed a system of working with plans, and long before his actual move into the new position, had become a goal setter and achiever. He gave the best effort that he possibly could to his previous job, even though it was not totally to his liking. He made it enjoyable, and then it became possible for another job of larger magnitude to come his way.

... AND THAT'S THE WAY IT REALLY IS!

By simply going into action with a plan for one weekend, Frank broke the bonds of inertia and was rewarded with a lifestyle that was successful and fulfilling.

Goals must be acceptable to the goal setter. Can you see how Frank would not have been able to accept the magnitude of his destined goals, had he known of them in advance? His mind could, however, accept the simple goal of planning a weekend. The point is, we must take those first small steps or we will never catch a glimpse of the larger benefits. Unless we go into action today, doing those things that are to be done by us, we will never know the beauty and the joy of our future destiny.

Everything that exists in your life, or upon this earth was first a thought in the mind of God. Look around you and observe the things that were manifested through the minds of the human race. The furniture, the building, the clock, the carpet, the television, the automobile. Except for things of nature, almost everything you can behold was conceived in the mind of man through the power of divine intelligence. Whatever you can identify with, in your mind, is almost sure to come into your experience, therefore, it is important that you identify with your goals.

It is extremely important that you identify with **what you want to happen**, rather than what you do not want to happen, or what has already happened.

DEVELOP AND "HONOR" A FLEXIBLE PLAN

Identification with what you do not want to happen will surely result in **exactly that**. What you fear most will appear.

We must also begin to identify with experiences and events that are beyond what we think are our present abilities. The potential is there. The potential for fulfillment is within each one of us.

Almost every Sunday, a very bright and talented young medical student was seated in the back of the sanctuary. Now, if you know anything about becoming a physician, you know that you have just broken off for yourself a healthy chunk of goal-setting. It is a way of life that consumes you for years and years, but a marvelous thing takes place if you are accepted at a medical school.

They have a plan for you. In fact, they have every hour planned for you, every day! They move you forward in increments of time and ability. They immerse you in a system, in a language, and in a philosophy. In time, you become the thing that is your goal. You actually become it. The moment you become a doctor, every fiber of you is a doctor. Somewhere along the way, you became so identified with your goal, that you became the consciousness of the goal and you became the goal.

I once had occasion to spend about three hours with a surgical specialist, and I asked him about his experience of becoming a surgeon. He said, "It takes a lot of time, you know."

... AND THAT'S THE WAY IT REALLY IS!

I asked him if he was frightened the first time that he opened an incision and he said, "No, it really doesn't happen that way. For example, I train young physicians to become surgeons. The first time we let them into the operating room, we have them stand over there in the corner. Sometimes they faint. I didn't exactly faint during the first major surgery that I watched, but I sure felt like it."

"After the candidates have watched from a distance for a while, we allow a closer surveillance, and in time, we permit participation by inviting them to hand us instruments. A few days later we will unexpectedly place the scissors in someone's hand and say, 'Here, cut this suture.'"

"Then one day when a particular student is ready, we will offer them the scalpel and say, 'Here, open at this point,' and the fledgling will make his or her first incision. The budding surgeon is prepared for this major step because the consciousness for it is already developed." Can you begin to see how medical school and many other fields of endeavor consist of a series of goals?

Now suppose you went into real estate or some other profession that required a self-motivating consciousness. The plan is not there for you, but the principle requires the same **discipline**. Discipline, you will discover, is essential for success.

CHAPTER XIV

DISCIPLINE

Medicine, among other things, is a discipline, is it not? It requires a participation. It requires a controlled activity on the part of the individual who will be a part of that experience.

Failure is also putting together a success system. Did you know that? All people who fail have put together a success system with which to fail. Losers can fail as consistently as a winner will succeed. If failing while in their present geographical location seems somehow not good enough, a non-winner will move somewhere else and fail even more completely. Give a non-achiever another assignment and that person will show you exactly how to fail, swiftly and quickly. In fact, the unfulfilled will even predict to you exactly how they will fail.

People who fail want successful people to come and rescue them, and weak people want strong people to come and take charge. The irresponsible want the responsible to bring order out of the chaos that they have created. This can never be.

... AND THAT'S THE WAY IT REALLY IS!

Being undisciplined is a way of secretly calling for rescue and stalling for time until help arrives. Unfortunately, there can never be enough help to rescue the undisciplined.

If you will go out into your success experience, it can only be with a disciplined mind. Discipline is a word almost all of us have shied away from. We have thought of discipline as something that has been imposed upon us from some external source. Most of us have been told by our parents, teachers, or peers, to "do this or do that," whether we like it or not.

Discipline, as I will use the word, means inner control. You become your own new frontier. You realize that the only thing you have to take charge of in this universe, is your own mind and your own life.

Discipline is not obedience to an external power, but to an internal system that you have chosen for yourself. You know that you must have a system if you are going to succeed, but you **must practice** that system. Unless you take yourself by the back of the neck and the seat of the pants, you will not do it.

Discipline **simplifies** your life and enforces clean decisions. Discipline is remembering what you really want. Do you know how difficult it is to remember today, what you promised yourself you were going to do yesterday? That is discipline. It is the remembering and the executing.

DISCIPLINE

Amy Gross wrote, "A cutting edge, discipline. It divides the people I know into the sleek and the nervous. With discipline, one has a handle on life. Without it, one is constantly burning one's hand on the pot."

Dr. Robert Schuller wrote, "Possibility thinking makes miracles happen, and the greatest power in the world is the power of possibility thinking."

If your dream has come from God, then you need only to exercise this miracle-working power and you can reach any seemingly unattainable goal.

At this point you are about to confront your biggest problem; "You." The hardest part is to now make yourself really believe that the apparently enormous goal you have established for yourself is somehow, someway, attainable.

You say, "I believe" and you immediately have an uninvited thought in your mind that says, "Almost."

I say, "I believe, but God, please help my unbelief! Help me to be disciplined in my thoughts. Help me to bring forward each day into consciousness, a memory of what I believe. Then, help me to increase my belief. Help me to increase my feelings and thereby expand my belief even more."

... AND THAT'S THE WAY IT REALLY IS!

You can achieve any goal you have established, as long as you let go of your impossibility thinking. All of us, have had this "stinking thinking." Impossibility thinking will cause you to do nothing about your goals. You will not go into action. You will not do what you need to do, and consequently, you will fail.

A reporter aired a story that was sent to him by a person we shall call Miriam. For twenty years, Miriam had dreamed about taking a vacation to Hawaii. Oh, how often she had thought about it. It was her heart's desire, but she gave herself a long list of reasons why it would not happen.

She thought, "It is too expensive and I have no way of overcoming the monetary problem. I have a family which surely I cannot leave at home. At the dealership where I am employed, I am the office manager and most certainly they cannot do without me for the two weeks it will take for the trip." She was an impossibility thinker. (And a very good one at that!)

Then she learned about goal-setting and wrote to me in a letter. "Last week, I wrote down the goal of vacationing in Hawaii. I visualized it. I expressed my gratitude for it and actually had the feeling that, now at long last, I was going to Hawaii. I was so excited about going to Hawaii that I couldn't stop thinking about it."

DISCIPLINE

"Last night, just one week later, my employer **called me at home** and said that our company had won a trip to Hawaii in January. For eight days, all expenses were paid and the company wanted **me** to go!"

"Jack, I have worked in dealerships for the past twenty-five years but never have I known a dealer to offer a trip to a female office manager. This was indeed God's answer to my dream and my desire. I am so grateful."

For twenty years, she exercised her impossibility thinking and she achieved her exact goal. Her goal was not to go to Hawaii. She did not go because she said "I cannot go. I want to go, but I know I cannot," and so, she did not go. The mere wanting of something, regardless of how strong the want, does not suffice for the accomplishment of a goal. Another element must be added and that element is **belief**.

Within hours or days of the time that she began to believe in possibility thinking, it happened out of the blue in an extraordinary way. Is that unusual? Not really. Dr. Maxwell Maltz wrote in **"Psycho-cybernetics,"** "Your built-in success mechanism must have a goal or target. This goal or target must be conceived as if it were already in existence. It must exist now either in actual or in potential form."

... AND THAT'S THE WAY IT REALLY IS!

Your success mechanism operates by steering you to a goal already in existence within the substance of the universe. The automatic mechanism is oriented to **end results**, which in this case, are goals.

CHAPTER XV

THE "MEANS WHEREBY"

What follows is another important concept. Do not be discouraged because the **"means whereby"** to bring about the accomplishment of your dreams may not be apparent. In other words, you do not have to know **how** this will happen. You only have to know that **it will happen**.

It is the function of the automatic mechanism to supply the "means whereby," when you supply the goal. Think in terms of the end result and the means whereby will take care of itself. You and I have been so caught up in the means whereby that we lose sight of our goal. Conversely, when we lose sight of our goal, we become caught up in the means whereby.

A goal is something you establish, bring into the now consciousness, and know that its accomplishment is the responsibility of divine intelligence or a power greater than yourself. Concern about the creation of the means whereby is not important. Do not let it be important to you, because giving it value will cause you to become an impossibility thinker.

... AND THAT'S THE WAY IT REALLY IS!

Do you understand what I am saying? If you want to practice impossibility thinking, then try to figure out how you are going to fulfill your goal. You cannot do it.

Keep your eye on your goal. Know that the means whereby will come to pass if you do your part. In the most amazing way, you will experience your goals. It will happen to you. It always does.

Assume the feeling of the wish fulfilled

In the days of Jesus, the language of the time was Aramaic. It was spoken and written entirely in the present tense. Consequently, it had no past or future tense. For example, the Lord's prayer is written in the present tense. You should always feel your goals in the **now** tense.

In Mark 12, verse 24, Jesus said to his followers, *"What things soever ye desire, when ye pray, believe that ye receive **them** and ye shall have **them**."*

Assume the feeling of the wish fulfilled. Bring your feeling into the now moment, into the present tense. Goals are not future tense. Do not think of your goal as something you are going to achieve, because if you are going to achieve it, you never will.

Your goal is something that is already achieved. The end result is there, and the whereby will take place in its proper time.

THE "MEANS WHEREBY"

Someone asked me if you should give specific dates for the completion of certain goals. The answer is yes, if you wish to work in a three-dimensional way.

There is a better way and in order to experience the better way, you will need to understand something about the fourth dimension. Our human thinking takes place in the third dimension that contains within it, the ingredient of time.

If you believe you are a three-dimensional person, then you will have to set dates for the completion of your goals, but in actuality, you are a fourth-dimensional being. This means that you transcend the realm of normalcy, and you have access to that fourth dimension Jesus called the "kingdom of heaven."

The fourth dimension encompasses and embraces the other three dimensions. In it, time does not exist, nor does space as we know space, nor do conditions. It is unconditional.

What is the only state you know of that contains no time? The answer is, **now**. I am in this now moment. If you take your goals and your dreams, feel them as already accomplished and see them as already done, it is absolutely amazing how their completion will come to pass.

A number of years ago, I was about to buy a boat for my three sons (and myself), only to discover that a large business group to which I belonged was raffling a boat, motor and a trailer. My sons and I decided to use these ideas to see if we could win the boat.

We purchased about two dozen tickets. (There were many thousands sold all over the eastern half of the United States.) For about two months, I visualized myself in that boat. I would ride down the lake with the wind blowing by my face, and I would hear the whine of the engine as it propelled my sons and me across the water.

I could see myself water skiing and I could feel the thrill of jumping the wakes. I even made it in the air from one wake to the other. My feelings were so vivid that one day I almost fell out of the boat! The vision startled me back into the now moment and I thought, "You are going to have to drive that boat more safely than that, Jack."

It was a **real** experience. I knew I had to get out of time and into the consciousness of now. I do not have to tell you what happened but I will anyway. We won the boat!

I was walking down a long beach in Florida the night before the drawing was to take place, (actually it was more toward the morning). As the sun came up, I was singing in the top of my mind, Sweet Hour of Prayer. (I sing much better in my mind than ... well, you know.) I wish you could have heard me singing in my mind. In that moment when the sun came up, I knew that this boat would be called, "Sweet Hour." I accepted it as fact, went back to the motel and told my three sons that the name of the boat would be, "Sweet Hour."

THE "MEANS WHEREBY"

That evening we won the boat, but the feeling of exaltation in having this experience was more important than the boat.

Two years after that, I was at the same annual meeting. Someone heard the story of the boat and said, "Jack, can you do that again? If you did it one time, you ought to be able to do it again. Why don't you prove it?" A drawing was about to be held for a television set and the thought occurred to me, "Well, why haven't I been working on the television set?"

I put my mind to work. I sat there visualizing the television set and got the feeling. I established the image out of time and I saw the girl that was to pull the ticket. I saw her reaching in and pulling out one of mine. Now this was some time ago, but that television graced my office for many a day.

We live in a magnificent universe which responds to our desires and to our now moments of consciousness. You live in a sea of infinite intelligence which will take the form and shape your consciousness will give it.

You will have a plan and you will work with your plan. You will be amazed at how a super intelligence will work with you to help your plan unfold.

By all means, set goals beyond your goals. As you move forward into exciting new events, set other goals.

... AND THAT'S THE WAY IT REALLY IS!

As I have suggested before, there will be obstacles in your path. Some of those obstacles will be in the form of people — people who you have known for a long time — people you thought were your friends. They will not want you to achieve your goals. If you are in movement, if you are in motion and they are static, they cannot stand to be left behind. They will want to pull you back into the static condition, into the condition that is their goal, and into the state that they occupy.

Frequently, your experience will require you to set these people free. If you are not ready or capable of eliminating from your life, all things that stand in the way of obtaining your goal, then be prepared to fail. You might as well let that goal rest, because you will not achieve it.

Jesus said, *"If thy hand offend thee, cut it off: If thine eye offend thee, pluck it out:"* You must be prepared to separate yourself from anything that is not consistent with your goal, whether it be an idea, a thought, an emotion, words in your vocabulary, or people in your life.

CHAPTER XVI

ENTHUSIASM!!

Ralph Waldo Emerson was only one of hundreds of great voices who said nothing great was ever accomplished without enthusiasm.

Enthusiasm. Oh, how I love the word. I had a friend, Larry, who signed his letters, "Enthusiastically." Can you not feel it? He lived his life enthusiastically. How are you living your life? Enthusiastically!!! Or enthusiastically???

Larry is a person with a winning consciousness. A person with this winning consciousness can easily change where they live. They can go anywhere in the world and immediately begin again to demonstrate success.

About three years after Larry moved to Oregon, I received a telephone call from him. It was in the same week that I had used Larry as an example in a goal-achieving lesson.

... AND THAT'S THE WAY IT REALLY IS!

He said, "I have some exciting things I want to share with you, Jack." Many of his goals were coming into focus and he was eager to share the news of his success. For example, his Dale Carnegie sponsorship had become number one in the world in the area of percentage of quota. He was on the top, the leader of all of them.

At the age of nineteen, Larry had become involved with the ideas of success as a result of curiosity. One evening he quietly slipped into a sales and marketing executive rally in Cleveland.

He was just a kid, and while seated there listening to the speakers, he thought, "Gee wouldn't it be great to be up there on that platform!" His mind had caught a fish and it happened to be a big one. Twenty years later Larry had the most successful Carnegie franchise in the world. He is a loving, sensitive, exciting, enthusiastic man who helps many, many people discover and develop their potential.

Larry discovered early in his life that, in the process of attaining success, one discovers you cannot do it by yourself. Not only do we need the help of our contemporaries, other people like ourselves, but we need help from a power greater than ourselves. The knowledge that we have help from a power greater than ourselves, produces in us an enthusiasm that strikes a sense of awe in our observers.

ENTHUSIASM!!

Enthusiasm turns on the switch that connects you to the power of the universe. Many a person has lost their goal when they lost their enthusiasm for it. As you move forward, maintain your enthusiasm. Generate it, increase it, and praise it. You will always be able to accomplish your dreams if you maintain your enthusiasm.

Possibility thinking is the maximum utilization of the God-given power that is resident within you. It is knowing all things are possible through him who is within you. Possibility thinking makes it possible for you to say, "If you have seen me, you have seen God going into action. It is my Father's good pleasure to give me the kingdom and I am going out to find it, **enthusiastically and with excitement!"**

Possibility thinking is believing God has unlimited financial resources and unlimited intelligence to achieve any goals. Possibility thinking is simply opening your mind to God's mind, and opening your life to the power that will surge through you.

God performs miracles in the lives of people who, being unafraid of failure and public embarrassment, move boldly and bravely forward. They attempt big things for themselves and accomplish their goals, but they always remember that the credit and the glory go to God.

... AND THAT'S THE WAY IT REALLY IS!

If you would like to achieve big things for yourself and for the people you love, know that nothing is impossible. You are the rich child of a loving Father, and all that the Father has, is yours.

CHAPTER XVII

WHAT YOU GIVE IS WHAT YOU GET ... "TO KEEP"

You get lots of material possessions in life. Have you noticed how many of them you do not keep? Have you noticed how many things have a tendency to slip through your hands? You get them, but you cannot keep them. They are not yours. You only get to keep what you can give, or as Vrle Minto says, "You keep the carbon copy."

This universe, this loving universe, this exquisitely responsive universe, is always sharing itself with us. It shares all of itself, holding nothing back, and it requires that we be like unto it, because we have been created of it. We are of its essence.

What the universe does, we must also do, and consequently, we cannot hold anything back. You can only keep what you can give. Security has never ever been achieved in the acquisition of persons or things, but only in the sharing.

Frank Lawbuck wrote, "These rivers of living water carry everything with them." He is not talking about the water that is of the earth, the water that we drink.

... AND THAT'S THE WAY IT REALLY IS!

He is talking about the streams of spiritual energy flowing through universal power and love.

If man can allow his mind to be wide open so that he does not block God, all the power and love of God's infinite heart can flow through him.

It is not until we become a channel for this living water, its essence, its power, its creation, its form flowing into us and through us, that we feel the satisfaction of giving and receiving. It is the flowing through that changes our destiny and gives us the security we seek. Never can we hold on to this water, because if we do, we block God.

Ultimately, dams we may have formed must break and allow us to become channels. In the channeling of these universal energies, we find our strength, our peace, our destiny, and our security.

I have looked in many sources of information about goal-setting, and nowhere have I found information about the above principle.

Some years ago, Joe Girard, the world's greatest automobile salesman, gave up selling automobiles and became an author. He was invited to be a guest on the "Good Morning Detroit" television show, with the purpose of discussing his new book **"How To Sell Anything To Anybody."** Joe was a failure by his own admission until the age of thirty-five. He then discovered a mechanism for success and in just fifteen years, made a phenomenal demonstration with his life.

WHAT YOU GIVE IS WHAT YOU GET ... "TO KEEP"

In the television interview, Joe was discussing a theory about the success in his life. He said, "You must have a mission in life." Now, mission was the word he used, but he obviously was looking for a better word. All of us, from time to time, have difficulty expressing ourselves with words that precisely convey our thoughts and ideas.

The host said, "Joe, you made lots of money selling cars, wasn't that your mission?" Joe said, "Yes, I made ten times more money selling automobiles than I am now making writing these books, but I must teach and help people experience what I have experienced. I must share what I have found. When someone later comes to me and says that their life has been made richer because of something they learned from me, that makes my life richer. It is more rewarding than money. I have more than enough money now, but I don't have enough of these other things to satisfy my life. A person needs to have a mission."

A woman, who saw the television interview, told me she had seen Joe's new book on the book rack in a drug store. She said to herself, "Oh no, not another self-help book," but she happened to open it up ... you know how we sometimes take a free peek before we put the book back on the shelf? What she saw when she opened it was a statement to the effect that, yes, you need to have goals in life, but you need to have goals for today. You need to have a plan of action for each day. It's not enough just to have general goals for your life. You need to condense that perception into a plan of action for today.

... AND THAT'S THE WAY IT REALLY IS!

Remember, in a previous chapter, we talked about a plan of action? We talked about going into action in this time compartment that you call today. It is interesting that this was exactly what the woman needed to read. She could not get the idea out of her mind.

She decided to take action and came up with a game plan for the next day. As a result, her next day turned out to be one of the most exciting and successful days she has ever had. She is not a salesperson, but she is a professional. Is it a coincidence that she should pick up a book about how to sell anything to anybody? Is it a coincidence that these ideas began then to work for her?

You must have goals because your mind is a goal-seeking mechanism. You need to have goals for your whole life, and you need to have a plan of action for today. You cannot have a worthwhile plan for today unless you have a mission. Furthermore, that mission must be larger and must be greater than merely the fulfillment of your own goals.

The word "mission" has among its definitions the thought of "a self-imposed duty," and comes from the Latin, meaning "to let go" or "to send."

I personally have a self-imposed duty and I freely share it with you. My self imposed duty is to go out into each day to do the best I possibly can to make this a better world in which to live. Is it presumptuous of me to have that kind of mission? I do not think so.

WHAT YOU GIVE IS WHAT YOU GET ... "TO KEEP"

To let go means to send. I have to let go and send myself out into this life to have a new experience. More than that, to the best of my ability, I must cause other people to have a better experience. As a result, I become less important and I am concerned more and more about you.

Concern does not mean worry. I know something about you that you may not yet have realized. You are going to make it. You may struggle a bit, you may go kicking and squealing through to your ultimate destiny, but you will make it. Life is rigged and it is going to take you there, whether you like it or not.

I have dried all my tears for you except for those of happiness. I will never suffer for you as long as I live, and I promise you that. You cannot call me on the telephone and get me to worry about you, or to be afraid for you, or even to feel sorry for you ... ever. I believe in you, more than you could possibly believe for yourself. I know you are going to get there.

If we are going to succeed in life, and I am sure that success is our primary goal, we are going to have to become responsible. Responsible not only for our success, but **responsible** ... meaning answerable for our own behavior. We must be able to be trusted and to be depended upon. We must be reliable and responsible to each other.

... AND THAT'S THE WAY IT REALLY IS!

Your destiny is important to me and the quality of your life is important to me. I know how Joe Girard felt when he was looking for a better word than mission. A word is needed to describe the desire that arises in the heart of each of us, the desire to share with others what we have found ourselves.

It is in you, this mission, this desire to **share**. You may not be so bold as to stand in front of a television camera as Joe Girard did, or to stand in front of a pulpit, as I do, and admit it. I will admit it for you.

I will tell you something else about yourself. I am going to lay a word on you that I'll bet you never have thought of, especially about yourself. I am going to label you a "philanthropist," a lover of people.

A philanthropist is one who makes the effort to increase the well-being of mankind, who makes the effort, who does the things necessary, who gives of his or her substance.

To love people is not philanthropy itself. Philanthropy is love going into action. Suppose that Jesus Christ had come to the earth to have his experience, and merely reported to us that God is love, merely reported that God loves you. That was all, just the report. There was no involvement. You were limited to just the idea that God loved you.

WHAT YOU GIVE IS WHAT YOU GET ... "TO KEEP"

It was not a love that was responsible to you and you could never connect with it. It was not going to dry your tears and be uplifting to you. It would not direct you, or guide you, or put your feet upon the path. It would not guide you along the way. It was just a love that loved you from a distance and "kind of waved its hand." That's all you got, a wave of the hand. What kind of love would that be?

The Love of which I speak is not of that nature. This love is like the love that a mother has as she goes into the room in the middle of the night and changes the diaper. It does for that little child that which cannot otherwise be done. That is the **least** activity of this love, and often we erroneously think, it is the greatest.

Oh how the universe loves you. It responds to you. It cares for you. It is a lover of people. If a philanthropist is a lover of people, then God must be a philanthropist. Why not? God created people to love, and has given them everything they can ever possibly desire or experience, providing they appropriate that experience.

We have mistakenly believed that "to appropriate," means to receive or "to grab a bunch and hide it from everyone." Or I will put it in a bank. Or I will possess it and you cannot have that which is mine.

... AND THAT'S THE WAY IT REALLY IS!

In reality, the universe has given all that it has to **each** of us, and therefore it requires that we share. It requires that we share even though the sharing **subtracts nothing from us**.

The universe requires that we be like unto it, therefore, we can only keep what we give away. You cannot be a qualified receiver unless and until you become a qualified giver.

CHAPTER XVIII

FORGIVENESS

An Asset? Or a Liability?

The first step in learning to give is to forgive. "To for-give." It is very important if we wish to make our demonstration. Most goal-setting philosophies do not understand this important principle. To put it in accounting terms, the ability to forgive is absolutely an asset. Lack of willingness to forgive is definitely a liability. It's like having a ball and chain attached to your life, constantly dragging you down, sapping your happiness and curtailing your progress.

The ancient meaning of forgive comes from the root word that means "to give" or "to receive." It is very important that we recognize this. In our modern language and psychology, we have separated the giving from the receiving and we have seen them as two different words, two different acts, two totally unconnected meanings.

Actually giving and receiving are a polarity, meaning they compliment each other, and neither is real or complete unless the other exists, simultaneously with it.

... AND THAT'S THE WAY IT REALLY IS!

If you would draw out of your universal bank account the substance, the energy, the love, the wisdom, and the power you need to make your demonstration, certain conditions must be met. You can only do so if, at the same time, you create a flow away from you.

In fact, you cannot create the flow of these substances toward you, unless you cause them to go away from you. You must create a vacuum, a void, a space into which the "new" may flow.

Now, in order to accomplish this, one must give up anger and blame. One must give in advance, or to state it differently, one must for-give. To give before you receive is to for-give.

You say, "Wait a minute Jack, you're playing with my mind. Who ever heard of giving before they received anything. It's not normal. It's not natural. It's not human." You are exactly right. It is not normal or natural and that is why we must learn to do it.

Jesus told a remarkable story with a penetrating message. It is a message that our mind does not wish to hear and the lesson is found following the familiar story of the withering of the fig tree. Jesus taught, *"Whosoever shall say unto this mountain, Be thou removed, and be thou cast into the sea: and shall not doubt in his heart, but shall believe that those things which he saith shall come to pass; he shall have whatsoever he saith."* You can say to any mountainous problem, rise up and fall

FORGIVENESS
An Asset? Or a Liability?

away, and your command will be obeyed, but one must have more faith in God than they do in the problem!

All that is required is that you really believe and have no doubt! Exclamation point. Listen to me! (Note the exclamation point.) You can pray for **anything**, (Underline for emphasis) and **if you believe you have it, it is yours!** (Underline again for emphasis, **and**, exclamation point.) Now hear this! When you are praying, first **forgive** anyone against whom you may be holding a grudge. If you have anything against anyone, forgive them so your Father in heaven will forgive you your shortcomings.

This principle of forgiveness is a primary requisite of prayer. The first law we learned was believing, really believing with all your heart. We now find that there is another law, one that is like unto believing, and one that must be honored and obeyed. That law is to forgive.

Some of you have not come into the phase of making your demonstration. You are successful in some areas, but some things simply have not worked at all. There is a lack of movement in your demonstration. It is not happening to you and I want to tell you why.

If you have negative feelings, if you have **anything** against any person or any group of people, any race of people, any class of people, anyone who died years ago, against God, or against yourself, then you cannot make your demonstration!

... AND THAT'S THE WAY IT REALLY IS!

Let me show you how God works, and prove to you that there really is only one mind. One morning when I was writing about this particular point, my telephone rang and it was a long distance call at five forty-five in the morning.

Here was a timid voice that was surprised when I answered and she said, "I did not think you would be there." I said in a joshing way, "Well, why did you call?" When she realized I was kidding, she said, "I've been listening to the prosperity lessons and I can't sleep." I said, "I hope the tapes did not keep you awake." She said, "Well, it wasn't your cassettes, it was some ideas that were there."

"I'm into this need and this activity of making my demonstration. I'm doing something about my life. I'm calm. I'm calmer than I've ever been in my life. I'm not depressed. I'm not depressed, Jack. I'm not depressed. I believe everything you say, but I can't get the feeling for it. As a matter of fact, I know that I heard God say to me, 'Judy, I did not create you in perfection so that you could manifest mediocrity.'" She said, "I know I heard that, but I still have no enthusiasm. How do I create the enthusiasm that is going to create my demonstration. How do I get started?"

I said, "Well, have you forgiven everybody?" There was a pause and I faintly heard, "Everybody?"

FORGIVENESS
An Asset? Or a Liability?

After allowing it to sink in a second or two, I said, "Everybody," and I suggested that we forgive them **all** right now, right then.

We proceeded to start through a unique process. I asked her to think about the great good that she would like to have in her life, to get a clear picture of all of the exciting things she was trying to achieve. I said, "Tell me when the picture is clear," and in a few moments, she said "It's clear, Jack."

Then I said, "OK, now give all that you have for yourself to **each** of those people, **especially** the one who has offended you in the worst way." I could hear her gasp for breath, and then I heard, "To him?" I said, "Especially to him."

"Give my good to **that** person?" It is not **your** good **until** you give it to that person. Until you give it to the **least** of these, it is not yours. It is not yours! You cannot get it to keep. Even if you should get it, you cannot keep it. You can only keep what you can give away.

In a little while, she said, "Wait a minute!" "I see. Forgiveness is the joy of demonstrating my prosperity without resistance to any other person prospering. In fact, to forgive is to give to the other person, in advance, what I formerly wished for myself, alone. It never occurred to me that I would be required to release my innermost desires and dreams into the lives of other people." "Boy," she said, "does that ever feel good to my spirit. Now I can feel the enthusiasm I was missing."

... AND THAT'S THE WAY IT REALLY IS!

At that moment my eyes fell to the open Bible on my desk and this is what I read to her:

"One of the teachers of religion who was standing there listening to the discussion realized that Jesus had answered well and so he asked, 'Of all the commandments, which is the most important?' And Jesus replied, "The one that says, 'Hear O' Israel, the Lord our God is one, and you must love him with all your heart and soul and mind and strength.' The second is like unto it. (Meaning equal to it) 'You must love others as much as you love yourself.'"

You must love others. You see, all the world loves a lover, but the universe gives to a giver. I said to her, "In order to succeed according to the universal law that cannot be broken, you must become a philanthropist, a lover of people."

She replied, "I love people." I said, "Now you are going to have a chance to prove it. As your demonstration is made and these things come into your life, you are going to be able to share them with all the people around you. You are going to be able to take a part of everything you get from life and give it away. No longer can your good be for you, and you alone. Your life must become a mission of sharing and of making the lives of other people a joyous, happy and prospering experience."

FORGIVENESS
An Asset? Or a Liability?

I have often been asked, "Is it right to pray for **things**?" Just this week someone asked me, "Is it really right for us to set goals for material things and then try to have God give them to us?" I said, "Try?" "If you do it right, you don't try — meaning to make a feeble or futile attempt. You do it! Your good happens. It is the law."

If someone says to you, "I will try to meet you tomorrow evening," you know that they are not going to make it. You do not even look out of the window, do you? I will try. I will make a feeble, futile attempt. Sometimes we kid someone and we say, "I'm doing the very best I possibly can. Don't you know how hard I'm trying?" Meaning, I am not really trying at all. We live in a universe of law that requires you either do it or you do not do it. Trying does not count in this universe. It simply does not count. You either do it or you do not do it.

Jesus once taught this story of tenacity to his disciples. Suppose you went to a friend's house at midnight and you told your friend that you wanted to borrow three loaves of bread because you had company. Your friend shouts down at you and says, "The door is locked and besides, why didn't you go to the market? I had to go to the market so why didn't you go to the market? I am not coming down to give you bread for your guests."

... AND THAT'S THE WAY IT REALLY IS!

Now, you hear what your friend has said but you keep knocking and you know, in time, he will come down because you persist in knocking. It does not make any difference why. You keep knocking. Eventually he will come down and you will get the bread, just because of your persistence. So it is with prayer.

Keep on asking and you will keep on getting. Keep on looking and you will keep on finding. Knock and the door will be opened. Everyone who asks, receives, and all who seek, find. The door is open to everyone that knocks.

Jesus continued to teach as follows. *"If a son shall ask bread of any of you that is a father, will he give him a stone? Or if he ask a fish, will he for a fish give him a serpent? Or if he shall ask an egg, will he offer him a scorpion?"*

Of course not. If even imperfect persons like yourself give children what they need, do you realize that your heavenly Father will do at least as much and give the Holy Spirit to those who ask for him?

The Holy Spirit means the whole spirit, the whole activity, the whole of God and because it is whole, it will give you what you need, and more.

Obviously, I believe in goal-setting and in releasing those goals to the spirit of God within us. It is when we feel His presence working with us, in our lives, that we experience the peace that passes understanding, and the joy that is above all ability to communicate.

FORGIVENESS
An Asset? Or a Liability?

God must be working on something, and what better thing for God to work on than goals that have been conceived by him through you. God and you mutually decide upon the goals which will be yours and then the intelligence that directs your mind will reproduce those things, providing you fulfill the conditions. One condition is to become a channel through which his power can flow out into activity. We are channels through which the Master Mind can express its powerful, loving, and beautiful essence.

I am placing such a high value on this idea of giving because it is rarely correctly taught in life. We have never been taught of the polarity of giving and receiving, and that is why our lives have not changed.

Most manufacturers of fine sound equipment include, in the controls, a method for repeating a sound track or a recording. If you do not change the settings, the equipment will keep playing the same selection over and over until it becomes so boring you can hardly stand it.

Your life is like that. Suppose that a long time ago you set a goal by not setting a goal. (We have already learned that if you do not set a goal, you have set no goal as a goal.) You created a certain kind of day as a pattern. You then discover that your pattern day becomes a week, the week becomes a month, the month ... a year. You put this safe pattern into your life and it just keeps playing over and over and over again.

... AND THAT'S THE WAY IT REALLY IS!

Now do you see why we need goals? Why we need to decide that, no matter how beautiful life has been, we must change the record. We must change it **over and over again**. Take your best recording and play it a thousand times. See how much you like it. Take your best day and keep living it over and over again. See what it will do to you.

Your best day really is the forerunner of the one that is superior to it. The better must follow the best because you decide the best is not good enough, that you are a dynamic expression of all of life. You reprogram your mind to bring into expression a new day with new events, new circumstances. It will be delivered to you and will become your experience.

We have been led to believe that our security lies in the acquisition of worldly goods earned through our own effort. Once things are acquired, we are to hang on to them for dear life. When we hold on to things, the flow that leads into us must stop. If it stops, it blocks the channel, and a channel, to be a channel, must be open at both ends. If we stop the flow of life from coming in, because we have not learned to properly send it forth by giving, then our success and security are caused to stop.

Circulation, not **acquisition and retention**, is where our security lies. "To conduct" means to become a medium or a channel for the purpose of conveying. It means to transmit. My friends, we must become

FORGIVENESS
An Asset? Or a Liability?

conductors in life in order to become valuable supporters of the supporting system of the universe.

This is the meaning of tithing, or giving of a tenth. The first tenth considered should be given to that which has supported you. The place where you receive your system of ideas of truth and of learning, the place where you receive your spiritual food, should be the benefit of that which you give.

There is a part of the good that comes to you, the substance that comes to you, that you must keep and put aside as savings. This also should be a tenth.

Then, there is a part that you will spend, and let's call that, the eightieth part or eight tenths. This portion we will call the principal. This is the part with which you support yourself, the part you use to pay for your food, your lodging, and the beautiful new car in your driveway. It is the part that provides the means to send your child to college, and the part that takes you to the Bahamas.

You and I also must learn to **give of ourselves**. If you will read **The Prophet**, it will say to you, "What have you profited if you give of your possessions?" It is when you give of yourself that you truly give. This does not mean that you are not to give of your possessions, that you cling to them. You give of them, yes, but you also give of yourself. For if you will give, you will get. The scriptures say so.

... AND THAT'S THE WAY IT REALLY IS!

Your gift will return to you in full and overflowing measure, pressed down and shaken together, in order to make room for more. Whatever measure you use to give, whether large or small, will be used to measure what is given back to you. In other words, you can never really keep what you want, until you learn to share it, until you no longer want it for yourself alone. All that you can keep is what you give away.

You have heard it said that the meek shall inherit the earth. Thomas Clark wrote: "The generous inherit the universe and as for me, I choose the universe."

There was a time when my life changed so dramatically that I cannot describe it to you. For weeks and months I pondered, what is it that has brought this to pass? I hungered to know and one night it was revealed to me by the Lord of Love.

A moment along the way when I had given up all hope for myself, I shared my meager possessions with a person I never saw before and will never see again. In that moment, the law fulfilled itself. It can never be broken.

Why is it more blessed to give than to receive? Because as you give, you are placing your own "order" and the law of love will fill it, heaped up, pressed down, and running over. Go out to give yourself away. The more you give, the more you will become.

CHAPTER XIX

THE MASTER MIND PRINCIPLE

"For where two or three are gathered in my name, there I am in the midst of them."

— Matthew 18:20

Robert Lewis Stevenson once said, "An aim in life is the only fortune worth finding, and it is not to be found in foreign lands, but in the heart itself." A definite chief aim, a purpose, a reason for living, goals, all these things would be without value unless we have the **ability to implement them**. How would it be if you could dream, but not possess the mastery to demonstrate those dreams?

We live in an awesome, wondrous, orderly universe, the laws of which are carried out with exquisite precision. There is a super mind. There really is! It is a "Master" mind. It is a Christ mind, a super consciousness. The Christ consciousness is the mind that knows all and is able to accomplish all things. It can do this because it is one with the mind of God.

The mind of God seeks to express itself as the experience of man, and man has only but to fulfill the conditions. The few people who begin to suspect that they can establish a conscious contact with the Master Mind, still do not know how to make their personal connection with this power.

... AND THAT'S THE WAY IT REALLY IS!

First, I must know that I can establish this contact, but how? How am I, an individual, a puny little human being upon this earth, to establish a conscious relationship with the source of all good? By coming to understand the Master Mind principle, we will learn to establish this conscious contact with God. Furthermore, we will learn to establish a working relationship with God.

A successful woman came up with a beautiful idea that was very marketable, and she entered into a manufacturing process with the ultimate plan of marketing this exciting product.

Immediately, she began to run into a series of failures. The idea was great, but her venture was not very successful. In fact, this venture had cost her many, many thousands of dollars, draining her capital and her energy.

She was very upset when she finally decided to telephone me. We were no sooner into the conversation, when I could see that what was missing, was the Master Mind principle. An active participation in a strong Master Mind group would have, in all probability, prevented the problem she was currently experiencing.

She thought she could do something she could not do, and because she did not have the advice of other confident people, she stepped off into water that was above her head. The first thing that she needs to do is form her Master Mind group and find her way back to solid ground again. Therein will be the solution to her problem.

THE MASTER MIND PRINCIPLE

In his inspired book, ***"Think and Grow Rich,"*** Napoleon Hill wrote, "The Master Mind may be defined as coordination of knowledge and effort in a spirit of harmony, between two or more people, for the obtainment of a definite purpose." He went further to say that, "No individual may have great power without availing himself to the Master Mind."

Now notice it is not implied that you cannot establish a conscious contact with God without being a part of a Master Mind group. You can, and almost everyone does.

If you look back over your life, you will see that most of your spiritual experiences have been disconnected from what you perceive as your normal life. They have been filled with joy and beauty, but have no particular direct connection with your living experience. There have been beautiful moments here and there that you did not connect to goals, or to the need to achieve success.

What I am saying to you is this. I agree with Napoleon Hill. Great power can be accumulated through no other principle. Great wisdom concerning one's personalized goals cannot be expressed in any other way, on a continuing basis.

If you will analyze the record of any person who has accumulated a great fortune, even a small fortune, or anyone that has made a significant contribution in life, you will find, if you look deeply, that they have either consciously or unconsciously employed the Master Mind principle.

... AND THAT'S THE WAY IT REALLY IS!

If you know what you are doing, if you practice the Master Mind principle consciously, even greater power comes into expression.

Poverty and failure need no assistance. You do not have to help them. They are bold and ruthless and they are continually grasping at our hearts and expressing themselves in our lives.

On the other hand, riches and success are shy and timid. They have to be attracted, worked with and supported.

You have been instructed on how to set and organize a system of goals. By goals, I mean all of the things your heart desires to do, or to have, or to be. You have been shown how to transform those goals into image and word symbols, and how to put them into a form that your mind can and will accept. You have been shown how to arrange your goals into a logical form that will then become your definite chief aim.

You have been instructed in the absolute necessity for creating in your mind, feelings that are the equivalent of how you **would** feel if your goals were already fulfilled. By the way, how would you feel? How would you feel if all of your goals were already fulfilled?

Let's take a moment and generate within us the feeling of goals fulfilled. Let's get the feeling going right now. Let's get into the experience of the excitement. Feel

THE MASTER MIND PRINCIPLE

the absolute spiritual ecstasy that will be alive in your heart if a dozen miracles had occurred in this very hour of your life. How would you feel? Take time now to really get into your feelings, and then permit yourself the joy of dwelling in those feelings.

In this chapter, you will be instructed in the most important step that you have yet taken in the achievement of your goals. This step is not only natural, but necessary, if you wish to be a fulfilled person. As a spiritual being, you must demonstrate success; success not as I would define it, but as it would be defined by your own spirit.

You will be introduced to the electric secret of the Master Mind principle. I strongly suggest that you prepare to associate yourself with a group of special people of your choice. You will form this alliance for the specific purpose of creating the energy and the intelligence attained in a Master Mind group. This group will form and implement a planned course of action that cannot fail to achieve your goals and your definite chief aim in life.

I repeat that compliance with the Master Mind principle is essential. Do not neglect this compliance. I would also suggest that you seek an association with people who will tell you the truth about yourself, even and especially, if you do not wish to hear. Mere praise will not bring the improvement that you need.

... AND THAT'S THE WAY IT REALLY IS!

A person is already half defeated the minute he begins to feel sorry for himself. If you and I are left to our own devices, to make our own demonstrations, the time will come when we will feel sorry for ourselves. We will begin to spin an alibi with which we would explain away our defects and explain why we have not made our demonstration.

If you have formed the right Master Mind group, you simply cannot get away with this. Do not belong to any Master Mind group that will join you in settling for status quo. Do not belong to one that will let you explain away mediocrity, or one that will let you overpower them. Do not belong to one that will allow you to con them into believing that you are doing better than you really are.

If you belong to a Master Mind group that will permit you to do that, quit them immediately. Say to them, "I would not belong to any Master Mind group that would have a person like me as a member."

Before forming your Master Mind alliance, it is important that you decide what benefits you will offer the other individual members in your group for their cooperation. It is more important for you to understand what you are going to give them, than for you to understand what they are going to give you.

You are going to get your benefits from them, but are you sure they are going to get theirs from you? No one will be involved indefinitely without some form of

THE MASTER MIND PRINCIPLE

compensation. In this universe, there is no such thing as something for nothing. We work together in a spirit of mutual advantage and cooperation.

It is extremely important that you understand you must maintain perfect harmony between yourself and every member of your Master Mind group. The Master Mind group consciousness is canceled immediately whenever any disharmony begins to exist. I can promise you that if you fail to carry out this instruction to the letter, you can expect to meet with failure.

If you have been a member of a Master Mind group and it is not working successfully for you, check **within yourself**. The fault may be within you. The Master Mind principles always work when we are working in the spirit of harmony. You may find that you may not believe in the concept or you may not believe in one of your members. The Master Mind principle simply cannot function where perfect harmony does not prevail.

A Master Mind consciousness may be created through the bringing together, or the blending in a spirit of perfect harmony, two or more minds. These two minds coming together seem to form a ***Third Mind*** that may be appropriated and used by one or all of the individuals involved.

It is not that you create a third mind. You establish contact with the universal mind, an infinite presence that has always been there but is undetected by an individual when working alone.

... AND THAT'S THE WAY IT REALLY IS!

Remember that this mind, this Master Mind, will remain available as long as the friendly harmonious alliance between the individual minds exist. The moment that harmony does not exist, the Master Mind will disappear in the blink of an eye.

The simple reason is that in this magnificent universe, there is complete and perfect harmony from one side of it to the other side. A billion light years from here, nothing but perfect harmony exists. The Master Mind cannot and will not tolerate disharmony from any one of us. It will absolutely disconnect itself and withdraw from us.

It must not be assumed that a Master Mind power will spring forth out of every group of individuals who come together under the pretense of cooperation in a spirit of harmony. No group of minds can be blended into a Master Mind if one of the individuals of that group possesses any negative repelling thoughts.

Now, I do not mean that you have to be perfect all of the time. You know the kind of negativity about which I am talking. It is somebody who refuses to get fixed, and they like it that way. They are not going to be changed. If that kind of person is a member of your Master Mind group, one of you needs to leave immediately. Lack of knowledge of this fact has brought many a sincere person to defeat, thinking that the principle does not work.

THE MASTER MIND PRINCIPLE

The point is, the principle **does** work. Harmony is one of nature's laws. Without harmony, no such thing as organized energy, organized intelligence or organized spiritual activity can come to pass. Harmony is the nucleus around which the Master Mind develops power and if you destroy this harmony, you have destroyed the power growing out of the coordinated effort of a group of individual minds.

You can see this in many examples. For example, a marriage is supposed to be a perfect Master Mind relationship. Frequently it is, in the beginning, but then one of the partners begins to nag, to complain, to become negative or depressed, and what happens? Let one try to overpower the other over a period of time and the spirit of cooperation, that feeling of love and excitement that was originally there, is gone.

Have you ever worked in a company, an office, or an organization in which one or more people work with you at your level, who are extremely negative? Of course you have! You know what it does to the consciousness of the group, and you have often wished that management would do something to remove the offenders. They are destroying the harmony of the office. In time, you come to the decision that you really do not want to be there.

Henry Ford's gigantic success can be traced to the successful application of these very same principles. Henry Ford had all the self reliance that a person could have, but he did not depend upon himself for the

... AND THAT'S THE WAY IT REALLY IS!

knowledge necessary to move forward into successful development of the original idea that was his. He understood a principle and like Andrew Carnegie, he surrounded himself with men who supplied, and then implemented, the knowledge that he himself, did not and could not possess.

Henry Ford picked men who could harmonize in a group effort. It is a known fact that Henry Ford began his business career under the handicap of poverty and illiteracy. If you were to predict his success based on the facts apparent, there simply was no way for success to come to pass. Success could not happen with what he had working for him.

Within the inconceivably short period of ten years, Henry Ford had mastered his three major handicaps. Within twenty-five years, he had made himself one of the richest men in America.

Now, connect these facts with the additional knowledge that Mr. Ford's most rapid advances became noticeable from the time that he became a personal friend of Thomas A. Edison. You will then begin to understand the influence that one mind can have upon another mind.

Then, go a step further and consider the fact that Mr. Ford's most outstanding achievements began from the time he formed the acquaintance of Harvey Firestone, John Burrows and Luther Burbank. Here you will see the magnificent demonstration that comes to pass when giants come together.

THE MASTER MIND PRINCIPLE

This principle is available to every one of us. In your own life, you can make the same relevant demonstration. There is a super mind, a Master Mind, a super consciousness. It does exist and within it we live, move and have our being.

There are many, many examples of the Master Mind in the scriptures. Space does not permit extensive listing of them, but consider the following thought. Jesus Christ, the master teacher, did not perform a miracle until a short time after he had formed his own Master Mind group, by the calling forth of the twelve disciples.

The story is related in John, the first and second chapters. He formed a Master Mind alliance and then began the amazing series of events that were to follow. In time, all of his Master Mind partners accomplished each of the miracles that he himself accomplished. Did you know that? There was nothing that Jesus did that his disciples did not do also. They made demonstrations of the same order that were equal to his. This is a recorded fact.

You also are told by his teachings that you are as equal to him as his disciples were. In John 14, verse 12, Jesus says, *"He that believeth on me, the works that I do shall he do also; and greater works than these shall he do."* The Living Bible states, *"Anyone believing in me shall do the same miracles I have done, and even greater ones."* You have been told to practice these same principles of belief so that the demonstrations that are important and relevant to your life can come to pass.

... AND THAT'S THE WAY IT REALLY IS!

The Christ consciousness is the Master Mind. It is the mind in you that knows all things and is able to accomplish all things. The mind of God is in every one of us. Every person on this earth has access to the Master Mind, but the majority of people do not know that they can contact the super-consciousness. The very few who begin to suspect that they can establish conscious contact with the Master Mind, often do not know how to make their personal connection with this guardian spirit that lives within.

Did you know that all genius is the result of a person being in touch with this fourth dimension of wisdom and power? You are a genius discovering yourself. It might be difficult for you to believe, but it is true. The major problem in experiencing genius, is lack of belief.

Genius does not come from you. It comes through you. Webster defines genius as exceptional or transcended intellectual and creative power. Genius, the word, comes from a Latin word meaning "guardian spirit." You have within you that guardian spirit that I call the Master Mind. It is the power that molds and makes.

> *A man and his mind ever more takes the tools*
> *of thought, and shaping what he will,*
> *brings forth a thousand joys, a thousand ills.*
> *He thinks in secret, but it comes to pass.*
> *Environment is but his looking glass.*
>
> *James Allen*

THE MASTER MIND PRINCIPLE

God, is the Master Mind,
an infinite and responsive presence,
both visible and invisible,
one presence, one mind, one power is all,
and this one that is all,
is perfect life, perfect love, and perfect substance.
You and I are individualized expressions
   of God,
and we are ever one,
with this perfect life, perfect love,
and perfect substance.

How do we establish our conscious contact with the Master Mind? I suggest that you investigate acquiring my cassette lessons on the Master Mind principle because there are three hours of instruction on how to form and work with the Master Mind group. Sometimes it is best to hear our instructions as well as to read them.

Now for some instruction on how a Master Mind group functions. First you need to remember that the purpose of a Master Mind group is to establish a conscious contact with the universal spirit; to establish a conscious contact in such a manner that all members can experience an increased awareness of that spirit, and witness a demonstration of its power working in their lives.

... AND THAT'S THE WAY IT REALLY IS!

A Master Mind meeting is not designed for members to solve each other's problems. It is not a place for you to go and discuss your problems at length. Many Master Mind groups need to be reminded of this point. In fact, you go into a Master Mind meeting so that you can be elevated into the consciousness of the **solution**. You are lifted out of the consciousness of the problem.

Do not hear me say that you should not state your problem. State your problem. Recognize it but do not dwell in it. The chairman of the Master Mind group should not, and will not, let any Master Mind partners dwell in the problem, nor should the chairman allow any partners to become conversational.

If you get into a conversation in your Master Mind meetings, you are immediately back down into the third dimension. The Master Mind meeting must be a fourth dimension experience. Your aim is to be lifted out of normalcy into a super-natural, a super-normal state.

The ideal size of the Master Mind group is from two to six members. You can meet anywhere; in your home, a restaurant, your office, in the park, or at a church.

There should be a short sharing time at the outset to really get in touch with your spirit, but have as little conversation as possible. You want to get the feeling and the flow of the super spirit.

THE MASTER MIND PRINCIPLE

One person acts as a leader and opens the meeting by reminding the group that there is a Master Mind and it is taking charge of the consciousness of the group. The leader, or chairman, then leads each member of the group through each of the steps. **Each step is completed by each member before going on to the next step.** Members of the group verbally express their response to the step under consideration.

Step one is totally completed and accepted by the group. Then step two and step three, and as each step is accepted, the consciousness of the group is elevated to a higher degree.

If you have never had this absolutely magnificent and delicious experience, I urge you to become a part of a Master Mind group. I urge you to **feel the power**, the electricity, and the dynamic changes that will take place in you. Feel yourself be lifted up into that fourth dimension of timelessness and spacelessness. In this state, you receive insights into things that you cannot perceive in your normal condition.

All of the good things that have happened to me in my life have been the direct result of the Master Mind technique. They are the result of my consciously and deliberately making this principle a part of my experience.

... AND THAT'S THE WAY IT REALLY IS!

There are eight steps to the Master Mind consciousness:

1 **"I surrender."**

"I admit that, of myself, I am powerless to solve my problems, powerless to improve my life. I need help."

The ego has problems with the admission of personal powerlessness. It wants to be in charge but the first step to moving to the fourth dimension is surrendering the third dimension.

2 **"I believe."**

*"I come to believe that a power greater than myself, the Infinite Creative Intelligence, the Master Mind, is **responding** to me in a personal way."*

In the second step we are not only saying we believe that God exists. We come into the dynamic experience of a now moment in which, as a group, we believe that God is responding. The activity of God, the love of God, the attention of God is upon us all.

3 **"I understand."**

"I now realize that erroneous, self-defeating thinking is the cause of my problems, failures, unhappiness, and fears. I am ready to have my belief system completely altered so my life can be transformed."

THE MASTER MIND PRINCIPLE

In the third step we decide again to place ourselves completely under the influence of the Master Mind.

4 "I decide."

I make a decision to turn my life over to the care of the Master Mind, surrendering my will and false beliefs. I ask to be changed at depth.

Our will wants to remain in control. It always makes its exit kicking and squealing. We must make a firm decision that we are **willing** to be changed, at depth.

5 "I forgive."

"I forgive myself for all mistakes I have made. I also forgive and release everyone who has injured or harmed me in any way."

This is the honesty step. We release all of our mistaken judgments and negative emotions that we have directed toward ourselves or others. Many of us can forgive others much easier than we can forgive ourselves. Oh how we love to beat up on ourselves for our falling short. It is imperative that we release all inwardly directed blame and guilt. Then divine consciousness can flow through us. Divine consciousness is perfect substance, so how can we expect it to freely enter a state of imperfection. We must forgive ourselves.

6 "I ask."

"I now make known my specific requests to the Master Mind and my partners."

In this step, each member in turn speaks directly to the group and to the Master Mind. Any problem area is stated including healing needs, goals desired, or special projects that are important to that person.

Usually each person expresses one, two or three needs in a meeting, remembering that the Master Mind is not limiting itself to just those needs. A thousand miracles will be taking place, most of which have been unasked for by the participants. "Before you have called, I have answered," says the Spirit.

Jesus Christ was constantly making specific requests and specific demonstrations so that all around him could see the power of this magnificent intelligence working in an individualized and personal way.

While each individual is asking for guidance and help, each member of the Master Mind group gives that person their full and complete, loving attention. In your Master Mind alliance, this will be one of the most beautiful, dearest moments of your life.

THE MASTER MIND PRINCIPLE

You believe more for your Master Mind partners than they can possibly believe for themselves. You know that your belief is a channel through which the miracle is taking place. You know ... and the miracle happens.

Together, we can believe things that I cannot possibly believe by myself, and you can believe things for me as a group, that I would not dare imagine. We as a group can believe for you in a way that far surpasses your individual belief system.

7. "Gratefully Accepting."

"I joyously accept and give thanks, believing that the miracle-working power of the Master Mind is responding to my every need. I assume the same feelings I would have if my requests were already fulfilled."

A secret of miracles is in the acceptance of a miracle before it comes into what we perceive as the now moment ... into our consciousness. When we accept wholeheartedly while giving thanks in the now moment for that which we desire, the desire becomes a miracle that has already been granted.

8 "Dedication and Covenant."

"I now have a Covenant in which it is agreed that the Master Mind shall supply me with an abundance of all things necessary to live a success-filled and happy life. I dedicate myself to be of maximum service to God and those around me, to live in a manner that will set the highest example for others to follow, and to remain an open channel of God's will. I go forth with a spirit of enthusiasm, excitement, and expectancy. I am at peace."

When the earth was formed, a covenant was made as the creator of all life said, "I will never leave you, I will never desert you, I will always be there and I will respond to you. That is my contract with you."

Now, all contracts require an agreement by two parties and your part of the contract is to **believe it**; to believe it so completely in this present moment that you will think and act as though it is already done. You must believe it so much that you will give thanks even before you see it done.

Another commitment in the eighth step is the dedication of your life to be an example and to be a channel through which the Master Spirit may flow. When we receive, we must first give. Being an example is a form of giving.

THE MASTER MIND PRINCIPLE

You are channeling God's energy through you, causing others to recognize it and feel its effect.

Lastly, it has already been agreed that the Master Mind shall supply me with an abundance of all things necessary to fill my every need. This is accomplished without me making any of these things the objective of my existence. I will walk in peace.

Does it work? I wish I could share with you the scores of letters that have come back to me from all over this country since the Master Mind tapes were made available. Many of them are letters from people who had to go to great lengths to buy the tapes.

Comments like the following are typical of those received from people who are experiencing success using the Master Mind principle.

"What a dynamic process the Master Mind principle is! I thank you so much for sending such a powerful message. It has given me much more faith and strength than I ever believed possible. The energy that my Master Mind group and I generate is absolutely amazing. I know it works and produces positive results. Time after time, my Master Mind partners and I are thrilled by reports of success that previously seemed impossible."

... AND THAT'S THE WAY IT REALLY IS!

Use of the Master Mind principle allows us to recognize the genius that is within us. Genius means transcended intellectual creative power, and the word transcend means "to go, or be" beyond the usual limits. It means to outstrip or out do in some attribute, quality, or power. Would you not also like to demonstrate that you are a genius?

Transcend means to cross or climb over all obstacles in your path, to defeat all second force. You see, if you are in a Master Mind group, second force does not exist. Your Master Mind partners will not believe in it so it has no energy. Do you see why a Master Mind group is so important? It will dissolve second force. It will dissolve the resistance that would normally be in your life. It will cause you to perform at the genius level.

Transcend means to cause to go upward, to elevate or raise, to excel, to pass, to exceed the former, to escape classification in any accepted category. It means to transcend beyond the limits of experience and knowledge. It means to go beyond any experience, any condition, any circumstance that has ever prevailed in your life.

Herbert Spencer wrote, "Among the mysteries which become more mysterious the more they are thought about, there will ever remain the one absolute certainty that we are ever in the presence of an infinite energy from which all things proceed."

THE MASTER MIND PRINCIPLE

John Wolfgang VonGerfa wrote, "A mystic bond of brotherhood makes all men one." Together we transcend our human nature and together we rise above the limitations of the past. We experience an infinite energy and love from which our future good proceeds.

CHAPTER XX

BURNING DESIRE

If you are not experiencing the kind of life you desire, it is because your goals have not yet been clearly defined. You may want more, but you have not given yourself permission to define what more is. What is more? Have you told your mind what more is?

Desire is defined as "to wish or long for a request, a petition." Oh God, I desire a good life. Will you please give it to me? I hope ... I think ... well ... I'm not sure. That is not a desire! The emotion of desire must be turned into a **burning feeling of the wish fulfilled**. If you and I wish to make our demonstration, and I know you do, that desire has to become a magnificent, emotional obsession that continues to burn day and night. It must burn regardless of life's events, regardless of the heavy traffic or the heavy going within the framework of any twenty-four hour period.

The word desire comes from the Latin, meaning "from the stars." It means to shine. It means to investigate. If you have ever seen someone who was turned on with the true feeling of desire, they seem to almost be illumined, like a star. They do shine. They do radiate. There is a vibration that is there. You can see it. You can feel it. You are touched by the magnificence of that deep emotion.

The word desire also means "from the parent, or from the father." If you have been really working with your mind when writing down your heart's desires, you are in the process of discovering that they are from the stars. They are from the heavens, from the Father, from your higher self, from your source.

There is a deep, vital and eternal urge within each one of us to move forward and upward to better things. You cannot stop. You may rest for a moment, but you cannot stop. The urge for growth, for movement, for excellence, for joy, for excitement, is inherent in your nature and this urge must be released and thereby satisfied.

Releasing of this urge is not an intellectual experience alone. It begins with the intellect, but it can only continue through the releasing of emotions. Emotion is from Latin, meaning "to move out" or "to stir up." Every time you have ever been emotionally on fire, you have moved out into some new experience. "You stirred things up."

Take anger for example. It is a **negative** example. It will cause someone to move out and will stir up the wrong kind of activity.

BURNING DESIRE

When desire is on fire in you, you really will move out into the experiences for which your heart has longed. If we are going to have the experiences we want, we are going to have to stir up the activity of life.

It is possible for you, a spiritual being in this universe, to stir some things up, to work with your mind and cause some things to happen. Things will happen and produce, in an effortless way, the things that you have simply not had the ability to achieve or produce on your own.

I was talking to a teacher who conducts, among others, classes on goal-setting. He said, "Jack, why is it that more people do not demonstrate the success that is so readily available to them. For example, sometimes I will have a class of forty to fifty students and maybe only four, five, or six really become achievers. Only these few really do something about their fate. Some of the rest of them will go through the class with excitement, but they really do not permit their good to happen to them. Why?"

I suggested that most people have become static, meaning having no motion or emotion. They just stand there, waiting on the corner, watching life pass by, hoping that from time to time a little bit of it will rub off on them.

... AND THAT'S THE WAY IT REALLY IS!

Do you remember the play by Tennessee Williams, ***"The Streetcar Named Desire?"*** There actually was and is a streetcar named Desire in New Orleans. Let's imagine that we are going to take that streetcar named Desire and move it out of New Orleans and place it in San Francisco. Let it be one of the cable cars in San Francisco that goes from San Francisco Bay to the top of the hill.

Let's imagine that you can climb aboard that streetcar named Desire and ride for free, all the way to the top. Desire is a vehicle. It is a means of transportation. It is a vehicle that will transport you forward and upward inexorably into new and rewarding experiences. It will do things for you that could not possibly be achieved any other way. It will take you all the way to the top of "Nob Hill."

Imagine that Nob Hill is the land of your dreams. Nob Hill in San Francisco was originally the posh area in which the wealthiest of aristocrats built magnificent homes. Many of these people had made their fortunes by trading in the far East. In the Bible, East means within your spiritual self, but the far East in which they were trading was in the three dimensional world.

You and I are going to be carrying on our trade with the far east of ourselves. We are going into the Orient, into the East.

BURNING DESIRE

Nob Hill was originally "Nabob Hill" and a Nabob was a district in India. The English and Americans began to trade in India and many become fabulously wealthy. As time passed, they were called "Nabobs." In those days, the people in San Francisco who traded with India and made so much money also lived on Nabob Hill. Later Nabob Hill was shortened to Nob Hill.

How would you like to be a Nabob? You probably never thought of yourself in that way, but a Nabob is someone who was fabulously rich and had great power. A Nabob had the freedom and the ability to make decisions. They could walk forth freely into life, could accomplish, achieve, create and build. They could live on Nabob Hill. Would you like to be that kind of person?

Suppose you and I were on a streetcar named Desire that could carry us effortlessly up the steep slopes of adversity, through all the things that have been trying to hold us back. We will be riding higher and higher and as we climb that steep assent, we look out into a new view, a new vista, a new life, new dreams, new dimensions and new experiences.

The higher we would climb, the more you would have the feeling that you are a new person, one that is worthy, adequate, capable and responsible. As you climb higher, a complete new identity would take place within you. You would leave your low vaulted past. In a very short time, you would be in the land of your dreams. You would

... AND THAT'S THE WAY IT REALLY IS!

be in the reality of your new life. Would you like that? It can be your experience.

The problem with most of us is that, as we are riding that streetcar named Desire, the vehicle that will transport us to the land of our dreams, **we get off at the first corner!** How would you like to be on something that was destined to take you all the way to the top. At the first corner when the conductor stopped to let a little traffic go by, you saw your good as being right there and you enthusiastically embraced it. You jumped off the streetcar! Your **perceived** good got in the way of your **better** good.

Our low self-esteem causes us to stop before we are even started. That same low self-image can prevent us from getting back on track. It can prevent us from really recognizing our desires.

"Am I really worthy of my good?" I am sure that many of us have said that to ourselves at least fifty times this week. Is it really selfish to want more than I have?

What about the other people in my life? If I truly make my demonstration, I will leave them behind. They are not doing the things I am doing. Do I have the right to dream and to soar if my relatives and friends have never climbed higher? Who am I, to think I can do this? No one in my family has ever reached for these lofty heights. Surely I am limited by other factors like my education or my race or my sex.

BURNING DESIRE

This attitude is called "standing on the corner." Your goals are not going to happen to you while standing on the street corner of life.

Your demonstration begins with an awakened desire. I say, "Climb aboard and let's get going. Let's really get the feeling of movement!"

As you are reading these words, let's get the vibration going. This is an experience, not just the reading of words, and I am asking you to let your feelings begin to flow, to begin to manifest and exhibit movement in your inner being. If you were to have everything your heart desires, how would you feel?

You see, for most of us our present good has become the enemy of the better and we have to motivate ourselves. We actually have to talk ourselves into reproducing, in our minds, and in our feelings, an equivalent of how we would be, how we would feel, if our good had already come.

Most people keep looking back over their shoulders or standing where they are. They do this because where they are is the goal that they have demonstrated to this point. To do this is to be "double-minded."

In the letter of James, the first chapter, beginning with the second verse, *"Count it all joy, my brethren when you meet various trials, for you know that the testing of your faith produces steadfastness."*

... AND THAT'S THE WAY IT REALLY IS!

I am sure you have encountered various trials, have you not? Do you count them all joy? Are you glad that you did? Have you made your separation from the past? If you are still looking back, thinking that somehow your good is back there, or that your good is now limited and for some reason you simply cannot leave where you are, you are being "double-minded."

In James, we also find reference to a double-minded man. To paraphrase: *"And let steadfastness have its full effect that you may be perfect and completely lacking in nothing. If any of you lacks wisdom, let him ask God, who gives to all men generously, and without reproaching, and it will be given him. But let him ask in faith with no doubting for he who doubts is like a wave of the sea that is driven and tossed by the wind. For that person must not suppose that a 'double-minded man,' unstable in all his ways, will receive anything from the Lord."*

You cannot travel in two directions at one time and this is why desire is so important. It is the emotion that is going to move you forward, inexorably, toward your good and toward your goal. If you are going to turn back, you are double-minded. If you are going to look back, you are double-minded.

The world's great champion in looking back was Lot's wife. Remember Lot's wife? It was she who looked back and was crystallized into a pillar of salt by being double-minded. She was trying to remain where she was and that condition no longer existed. She was unwilling to move forward into the good, into the actual good that had been created for her to experience.

The past does not exist for us. The present is not satisfactory. Consequently, we have to move forward and desire is the vehicle that is going to get us there.

You have learned that everything man creates or acquires begins as a desire. Desire takes you on the first lap of your journey from the abstract. It takes you from the visions of your mind to the concrete, into the workshop of the imagination. In the workshop of your imagination, plans for the transition of the abstract into the real are created and organized.

Remember that you do not have to create or organize. This is something that will happen automatically as a result of the magnificent creative expression that you are.

If you can create a desire strong enough, you do not even have to see your goals clearly. They will automatically begin to take form and shape.

I cannot count the times I have seen a patient come through a medical challenge safely only to hear his physician say, "Nothing but his own desire to live has saved him. He never would have pulled through if he had not refused to accept the possibility of death."

... AND THAT'S THE WAY IT REALLY IS!

I have seen people live because they had an intense desire to fulfill something in their life that was not yet completed. They simply would not die until they completed that goal. I am sure we have all seen it happen.

I believe in the power of desire backed by faith, because I have seen that fantastic power lift people from lowly beginnings to places of power and wealth. I have seen it rob the grave of its destined victims. I have seen it serve as the medium by which men bounce back after having been defeated in a hundred, a thousand ways. I have seen it provide me with my own destiny.

Let me tell you a story about me. Many years ago I came to know, within myself, that I had to maintain a strong and continuing desire for the good that I wanted for me. That desire had to be the counter balance to overcome the negative emotions that existed in me for so long they were automatic and spontaneous.

I had to work to desire, to feel, to want the good life, and I had to work to believe in it moment by moment. I worked on these feelings and the work became an obsession, an emotional obsession, but a joyous obsession.

My life began to change in the most amazing way. It seemed that every time that I emotionally connected with a goal or a desire, whether large or small, that goal would develop as a reality in my life. In three decades, I cannot recall a single time this has failed.

BURNING DESIRE

The particular story I wanted to tell you happened a few years ago in Dallas. I had made one of the greatest demonstrations of my life. The finest position I had ever achieved was mine to enjoy. It was a position of some trust and prominence in that wonderful city. I was excited and delighted to be moving forward very successfully in that position.

One Friday, I returned from lunch and discovered that, through no fault of my own, the position no longer existed!

For about ten or fifteen seconds, there was an intense feeling of disappointment, of dismay, and of wonder. What have I done? How could this happen to a wonderful person like me?

Fortunately, I knew enough to catch the disappointment and to convert the feeling of disappointment to a burning desire for my good. I worked with my mind and said, "This too, is good for me. I must not judge by appearances."

You will understand if I tell you that for the next two or three days, I had to work very diligently to keep my thoughts and feelings under control. I am sure you understand these emotions.

It was on a Friday that the event occurred. Monday evening I found myself attending a meeting I would not have attended had not it been for the experience

... AND THAT'S THE WAY IT REALLY IS!

on Friday. That evening, I met the director of Unity Ministerial School, and almost instantly I caught a fish ... I landed an idea. I knew what my destiny was going to be. I knew it! The ministerial school director did not yet know it, but I knew it.

I saw this as more than a coincidence. Something happened in me. There was a commitment. The idea was totally accepted. I know that the change that had taken place on Friday was to move me forward into a larger and greater, more exciting and more rewarding destiny. I knew it and I also knew that this coincidence of meeting the director of Unity Ministerial School would not have occurred without that burning desire.

If I had fallen down into that state of disappointment or dejection or blame, who knows where I might be in life today? The commitment was made and it became a dedication. I can tell you that, from that moment to this, I have never doubted its rightness. I have never had one moment of wondering, "Is this what I am supposed to be doing?" I have never had to look back.

My life is so good I can hardly stand it. I look back and ponder that the event of Friday might not have happened, yet it had to happen. The worst thing that ever happened to me had been the best.

BURNING DESIRE

From time to time, someone will call me and say, with tears running down their face and sobbing on the telephone, "I lost my job!" I will say, "Great!" Are you surprised? Almost invariably, that person will end up better off than before this perceived disaster. All things work together for the good of that person who has a burning desire to demonstrate his good. Do you believe that? I will guarantee it. I promise it.

Dreams come true when desire transforms them into dynamic action. Ask this universe for its great gifts and then desire them. It will deliver them to you without fail.

There is a science of demonstration, there is a science of achieving your goals, and it is an exact science like algebra or arithmetic. There are certain laws that govern the process of acquiring that which you need, and **this science does not care who the scientists are!** Did you hear that?

The science of mathematics does not care who the mathematicians are. As long as you follow the rules you will get the results. As long as you know what you are doing, your answers will be orderly and correct. The science of demonstrating is the same way.

... AND THAT'S THE WAY IT REALLY IS!

Your demonstrations do not occur because you are a Christian or a Jew or an atheist. They occur because you know what you are doing and do it scientifically. You are a scientist of spirit. You are a spiritual scientist and if you will do in a certain way that which is supposed to be done, you will experience your desired result.

If a person fails to follow the rules, they will not experience the results and it is just that simple. No matter how hard you work or how eligible you might be for your good, unless you work with the right combination, you simply will not make your demonstration.

One of the last of our old ideas that we have to get rid of is the idea that poverty is virtuous. We have been taught there is a God that believes the universe will somehow be better off if we are kept poor ... that somehow you can serve the Lord better in a state of poverty.

Every desire you can possibly have is the effort of an unexpressed possibility seeking to come into action in your life. The desire could not be there unless it was a possibility trying to happen to you.

It can happen to you in a very important way. There is in this universe a mind substance. I am going to tell you a secret not all of you will believe. I hope you do. Right now, around you is a substance I am going to call "mind stuff." Early metaphysicians called it the "ethers."

BURNING DESIRE

It is that substance into which your thinking and feeling flow.

You have come to believe that thinking and feeling cause something to happen, have you not? There is an infinitely intelligent substance that is very impersonal. It cannot decide anything for you. It cannot make up your mind for you. It cannot decide where you are going to go, or what you are going to do, or what you need, or what you desire. When you think into it, and you are always thinking into it, your thoughts take form and shape.

Your thinking and feeling act in such a way upon this mind substance as to reproduce the pattern of what you are thinking and feeling in that substance. Now for a shocking thought. If you really believe this, it is going to impose a very important responsibility. You will become aware that every thought you think and every feeling that joins it is actually shaping this mind substance.

This is going to require you to be very responsible and to only think and feel those things that are consistent with your goals. You cannot just indiscriminately vacillate back and forth. You cannot become angry in traffic, or act in a way that is unseemly when you are with certain people. In every moment of your existence henceforth, you will be required to maintain a certain posture of your mind.

... AND THAT'S THE WAY IT REALLY IS!

Throughout every split second of your experience in this universe, the posture you have taken in your mind is affecting this mind stuff. This mind stuff is a thinking stuff and takes the patterns of your thought and reproduces them in your three-dimensional life.

A burning desire will be the vehicle that keeps your mind steady in its resolve to accomplish your goals. Desire will not allow those imperfect thoughts to travel through your mind and into the ethers. Ride the streetcar named Desire and stay with it until you reach the end of the line at the top of the hill. There your life's dreams are fulfilled.

CHAPTER XXI

INTO ACTION

Let a Winner Lead the Way

Now that you have set some goals, what have you done about them? Most of us will likely answer, "Not much." We have been waiting for something to happen. The problem is, something might not happen. Let us make something happen. Let us **make** our goals happen.

First I am going to ask you to remember that many of your goals are really new attempts to overcome conditions of previous non-achievement. In other words, you are attempting to overcome your previous failures. You have demonstrated a lack of success in the past, and there is nothing wrong with that. It is **past** tense.

Some years ago, a football coach gave this advice on how not to be a failure. He said, "When you are about to be run out of town, get out in front and make it look like you are leading a parade." In other words, ***go into action.***

... AND THAT'S THE WAY IT REALLY IS!

Let a winner lead the way. In fact, let a former loser lead the way. I like to follow former losers. Show me a former loser and I will show you somebody that will never quit moving. In the spirit of what old Satchel Paige once said, "They don't want to look back for fear something might be 'gainin' on 'em!" They want to keep going in the direction of their success and prosperity.

Some people who previously were life's greatest failures have become the world's most successful giants. If, so far, you have not been what you consider to be successful, so what? The world is in front of you. Inside your spirit is lurking another giant. You, also, can be successful and free your spiritual giant for the world to see.

Nothing restrains goal setters more than the knowledge that they will have to carry out their plans. When you and I start setting goals, even while we are setting them, there is something inside that says, "Whoa! Wait! Stop! Wait just a doggone minute! You mean I'm going to have to **do something** about these ideas? Do you mean I might have to change? Do you mean I might have to exert some effort?"

The plain truth is, yes, you will have to exert effort. You now have to go into action. You can read every self help book in the world, go to every lecture on self improvement, listen to every tape that was ever recorded, but unless you go into action, you will fail.

INTO ACTION
Let a Winner Lead the Way

To act, in my dictionary, is defined as the process of doing or performing something. It means to actuate, to motivate, to carry out an action, to operate or function in a specific way.

You have been told in the past that if you do not have a certain quality, you should "act as though you have it." "Fake it until you make it" is a phrase that is often used. The idea is fine but the word fake implies dishonesty. It implies that you do not have the belief. In reality you must also **believe** that you can make it.

Act as though you have it and you will. If you put the **feeling** of the experience with the actual experience, you will become the act-or. All of life is a stage and we are act-ors upon that stage.

Action is somewhat different from act. Action is a choice that **involves movement**. It means the state or process of acting or doing. It involves the transmitting of energy, force or influence.

If you would like to have an experience upon this earth, the idea that precedes that experience must be transformed into an act or an action. The energy that sustains and supports all of life, and all of life includes you, must be transmitted or transformed. It must become influential in a sphere of activity.

... AND THAT'S THE WAY IT REALLY IS!

You must transmit that energy into your sphere of activity. You must begin to act out the role that you have assigned yourself by virtue of the choices your mind has made.

Nothing you desire upon this earth can happen to you unless you go into action. Oh, how I resisted this concept when I was an early student of metaphysics! Somehow many young metaphysicians misinterpret the teachings and begin to believe action is not necessary. They come to believe that if your faith is strong enough, you can meditate on a thing and it will come to pass.

Now, meditation is very important, but I had the mistaken idea it was the end product. I thought that meditation, of itself, would solve everything. There was something in me, and I suspect that you will understand this thinking, that preferred to see an event and, as I meditated, to call it forth. I would call it forth with my eyes closed and then I would open one eye very carefully. I expected to peek out, only to behold the manifestation of my dream in all its magnificence. All this I expected to do without any other action on my part.

Oh how I loved metaphysics when I thought this was the way it really was. One night a voice came to me and this voice spoke to me clearly saying, "Jack, I have news for you! You must **go into action** because I cannot do anything **for** you. I can only do for you **through** you. Go into action, Jack! Go into action!"

INTO ACTION
Let a Winner Lead the Way

"A problem," said Henry Kaiser, "is only an opportunity in work clothes. People who face their problems, who try hard to solve them, will seldom fail. Often they will reap benefits they have no way of foreseeing."

I mention this quotation by Henry Kaiser because most of us seek guidance in self improvement by virtue of having been motivated by our problems. It is not our performance of excellence that spurs us to search. It is because we, for the most part, just are not doing all that well. We want to find a better way.

Years ago, two brothers, Thaddeus and Eurastis Fairbanks, were running a small hemp business. Their biggest difficulty was trying to weigh the hemp with the crude and inaccurate scales of that day.

The bundles of hemp were huge and the scales were small. Consequently, the bundles kept falling off the scale. Finally one of the brothers constructed a platform that focused the weight of the hemp on the center of the scale. The method proved to be superior and they were able to weigh their hemp with great accuracy. What happened after that came as a complete surprise.

... AND THAT'S THE WAY IT REALLY IS!

Many customers wanted to buy the brothers' scales more than they wanted to buy their hemp. As a favor to their customers, Thaddeus and Eurastis began to manufacture scales. Soon the demand for the scales became so great that they gave up the hemp business.

You have seen the name "Fairbanks" on scales since you were a child. Their opportunity grew out of a problem and the success of their enterprise grew out of seeking to find a solution to the problem.

Show me a problem and I will show you an opportunity in work clothes. I will show you a situation where you can go into action and reap the most amazing results. If you sit and look at the problem, opening your eyes occasionally to see if the answer has arrived, you will probably not be blessed with desirable results.

People who dream impossible dreams and strive to achieve them, raise the stature of all of us a fraction of an inch in the process, whether they win or lose. You are solving your problems because you have come to believe in dynamic and spiritual solutions. As you go into action in your life, your action enhances and reinforces universal mind and consequently, you enhance every other person who lives upon this earth.

To strive and achieve our dreams is the key. The world is full of dreamers but there is a shortage of strivers. Dreamers are not necessarily achievers.

INTO ACTION
Let a Winner Lead the Way

I was a dreamer but my dreams became fantasies. I withdrew within myself and tried to live in my dreams. I did not know about making my dreams come true as living experiences, and so dreams were a way to escape from the responsibility of living my life. This is fantasy and it is the wrong use of the imagination.

Dreamers who strive are achievers, and conversely, strivers who dream are achievers. Andrew Carnegie was such a person. He came to this country as an uneducated immigrant. His first job was as a bobbin-boy in a cotton mill, where he worked for a few pennies a day.

From there he went on to build a multi-million dollar steel empire. His influence went far beyond the steel industry. He has touched my life and yours whether you are aware of it or not. Carnegie believed that his tremendous success was achieved because he was always ready, willing and eager to share with the people who worked for him.

Carnegie knew that we simply cannot achieve our goals by ourselves. As he brought key people into his life he practiced the Master Mind principle. In addition, he always rewarded his associates in every conceivable way, including the reward of recognition. On his tombstone is inscribed the following epitaph, "Here lies a man who enlisted in his service better men than himself."

... AND THAT'S THE WAY IT REALLY IS!

As you and I move forward into our demonstration to achieve our goals, let us not lose sight of the fact that we will not achieve those goals by ourselves. This will be difficult to remember. We will need to surround ourselves with the right people.

We will need to be aware of that infinite, invisible, but ever present spirit of God that is the source of all energy and of all power. Carnegie was a man who understood and practiced these great principles.

One test of the emotionally mature person is that even though they are intensely occupied with their problems, they still remember that their associates have problems too. As you move forward into achieving your goals, do not lose sight of the fact that you are a key person in the implementation, in the achievement, of other persons' goals. There has to be reciprocity implemented by the sharing of your energy, your wisdom, your insights, and your love. Your absolute dedication must be given so that you can receive an equivalent in return.

By following the principles of sharing you will not be alone in your judgments of what to do, when to do it, and how to do that which is to be done by you.

A school principal received a telephone call one morning and the voice said, "Tommy Jones won't be in school today." The principal said, "Who is speaking?" The voice said, "This is my father."

INTO ACTION
Let a Winner Lead the Way

How many times have you and I tried to play hooky from life, from our responsibilities, from something that we deemed to be unpleasant? Is this not what kids in school have been doing since time immortal? Kids seem to have a contest in which each of them is trying to outdo the other saying things like, "I don't like school." "I hate my teacher." "I hate math." "I hate English." Well, life, too, is a school. Life is a very "high" school.

I dreamed of quitting school when I was in high school. My dream became my goal and I achieved my goal by becoming a high school drop-out. Now, suppose I had dreamed of graduating with honors. I am sure that goal would have also been as easily achieved.

As a result of the drop-out goal that was achieved, I had to go back to the school of life to learn the things that needed to be learned by me.

You and I are in school right now. In your real life situation, are you dreaming of dropping out? When you first awakened this morning, did the thought occur to call the principal? Did you say, "I'll call God and say, 'I don't want to be there? Count me out. Even if I am there, I'm not there. I'm not going to like it. I am not going to enjoy this thing that I am to do.'"

... AND THAT'S THE WAY IT REALLY IS!

Do you say, "If I could just be in Southern California I would not be a drop-out. I would enjoy my life." But life says to you, "Who is speaking?" You must ask yourself, is it the little me, or is it the great me? The little me is always trying to escape its responsibility. It loves not being a doer. It is a spectator in life. It is a griper, a complainer and it has already figured out why things cannot work ... except, of course it will work in Southern California.

If you are to become a world-class goal achiever you cannot afford to merely let things happen. If you seek success, if you wish to demonstrate your goals, you are going to have to make things happen. You are going to have to cause your goals to happen.

You will notice that I did not discuss action and tell you of the effort you would have to expend early in this book. I wanted you to mature a bit along the way. You have the power and the responsibility to make things happen. It really is a very simple process once you become willing to accept that the time has come for action.

Suppose that, for example, one of your goals is to get a better job. You do not like the job you have and you want a position that will allow you to express your many talents. You want a job that will ultimately be a better channel for the worlds goods to flow into your experience.

INTO ACTION
Let a Winner Lead the Way

What is the first action that you must take? Is it to play hooky? Is it to quit your present job because you are not going to work there very long anyway? Is that what you are going to do? Heavens no! Absolutely not!

The first action is to go into action. The first action is to go to work. The first action is to really go to work for the first time in weeks, months or years. You must **enjoy** your **present** job. You must decide, in advance, that you will enjoy it. After all, might not it be the last day you will spend in that realm of employment? Why not enjoy it?

The next action is to bring your resume up to date so it will describe the new you. There is a very beautiful woman who has been looking for a job for several months. She left a job that did not exactly fit her and she has had only one opportunity since. If she were to outline the job that would displease her most, this one opportunity would be a perfect match.

I asked her if she had brought her resume up to date and she said no. We talked a bit about the ingredients of a good resume. A good resume should be akin to the ingredients in a biographical sketch I wrote about myself, a sketch I used to send out from time to time for speaking engagements.

... AND THAT'S THE WAY IT REALLY IS!

In writing my resume, I thought, "Gosh, If I am going to write about myself, I am going to write something that will cause the person who reads it to become excited." In time, the Association of Unity Churches adopted the form of this sketch to become the standard that the association uses for promotion of ministers in the movement. If you are going to write something about yourself, make it good. You are a fantastic person and many possibilities exist within you, so make your writings accurate, but make them good.

I recently met a young man and was surprised to learn that he had been twenty-eight years in government service and had achieved a high position. He appeared to be so young I could hardly believe he had been in the service that long.

The years of service had taken their toll and he explained that he really did not like his job. Someone had mentioned to him the possibility of making a change.

He said, "I suppose you are going to tell me that I am supposed to leave my job." I replied, "Quite the opposite. I'm going to tell you that I would urge you to go to work, on your job. Think about it. You only have two more years. Enjoy every exciting moment of it so when you leave you will leave from strength and dignity."

INTO ACTION
Let a Winner Lead the Way

"You will leave with power and move out into the equivalent of the action that you demonstrate **where you now are**. If you move from inertia you will be carried into that equivalent in your new life. The quality of your present action will determine the nature of your new experience."

From one of the western states, I received a letter from a man who has listened to our Master Mind Principle tapes. In his letter he told me how wonderful the tapes were, and that he has started a Master Mind group with some other beautiful people.

He went on to say, "I've only one question to ask you. I have been an employee in government service for some twenty-three years and I am not happy with my work. It is not pleasant. I am at the wrong place and with the wrong people. In listening to your Master Mind tapes I began to wonder. Can an ordinary person become rich simply by being in the Master Mind?"

In other words, he was saying, "Can I give up my job? Can I stop working and become rich? I don't like where I am. Can I pray about wealth and become rich? Can I practice meditation and have it bring to me all those things that I desire in life?"

... AND THAT'S THE WAY IT REALLY IS!

Of course, you know the answer to his question. In the first place, an "ordinary" person cannot achieve anything of consequence. What can an ordinary person achieve? Only ordinary things. You must become an extra-ordinary person.

Stop trying to be ordinary. There is nothing special or desirable about being ordinary. In fact, it is totally unacceptable. You are an extra-ordinary being who must go into motion, into movement so that you will draw to yourself the equivalent of yourself. You have become an energy field that magnetically draws you to that which you are.

I understand how this ordinary person of a man feels because I once felt that way. I wished that I could meditate and open my eyes only to behold that my answer would be there.

What this beautiful man needs to do is to go into action where he is. He must love where he is and what he is doing. He must become a blessing to the other people who are in his present life and in time he will become rich. New channels of opportunity will open and abundance will be his. Abundance will come as a reward for excellence, not for being ordinary. It will come as a reward for action and as a reward for service.

INTO ACTION
Let a Winner Lead the Way

I received a call from a woman who does not come to my church, but has heard of the work that we do. She has a problem with relationships, especially her marriage, and her goal is to find a solution to her marital problems. She is very sincere but unhappy and desperate. She wanted to know if I would talk to her husband and try to get him changed. I said, "Can you get him to come to church?" (I pretty well knew what her answer was going to be.) She said, "I can't even get him to go to his own church, how can I get him to come to yours?"

I talked to her about making some changes in her life and she said she was afraid to take action. She said, "I am afraid I will lose my marriage."

I said, "You don't have a marriage. The relationship you have described to me is a non-condition. How can you lose what you do not have?"

Have you noticed the inertia that overtakes our minds when we want something to happen outside our energy field, to produce our desired result? Because we expect other forces to solve our problems and change to take place everywhere but in ourselves, our minds become complacent.

... AND THAT'S THE WAY IT REALLY IS!

Let me tell you a true story that happened some years ago to one of my Master Mind partners. This wonderful person and his wife of some twenty years had grown apart many years ago, but continued to live together because of the children.

When the children left home the non-marriage became quite visible. It was very, very debilitating and he was looking for answers, but he was looking for answers without change.

One day following a Master Mind meeting, he came to my office and we talked about his going into action. I pointed out to him that he had three possible alternatives.

One was to live as he now was and he replied that the present condition was unbearable. One alternative was to fix the present condition and he said, "She will not change." The other and final alternative was to leave. He said, "I can't bear it. I've had this wedding band on my finger for twenty some years and I just can't bear the thought of it not being there." He walked out of my office with nothing resolved.

To my astonishment he came back about an hour later and had sawed off the wedding band. He went into action. It was rather drastic but into action he went. Can you imagine how difficult it was for him, and how frightened he was at the consequences of his actions?

INTO ACTION
Let a Winner Lead the Way

He took his wedding band home and showed it to his wife. She was shocked! Stunned! She was startled and **she** went into action. As long as we accept an unacceptable condition by waiting for a moment yet to come, waiting for an event, a circumstance, an eclipse of the sun to rescue us from that condition, we cannot move from our agony. We cannot escape our distress.

Would you believe that within several weeks this couple fell so madly in love that they looked like honeymooners. He had upon his finger a new wedding band, but what is more important, he had a new marriage in his life. He had a new marriage because he went into action. He took action and was willing to experience the consequence of that action.

"My dreams are worthless. My plans are dust. My goals are impossible. All are of no value unless they are followed by action. I will act, now!" Thus said Og Mandino in the ninth scroll from his best seller **"The Greatest Salesman In The World."**

Action is the opposite of procrastination and to procrastinate, in Latin, means to put forward until tomorrow. How many people do you know who put their lives forward until tomorrow?

... AND THAT'S THE WAY IT REALLY IS!

It is not important that you know of people who procrastinate, but it is important that you recognize this evil for the devastation that it creates. It is important that you recognize this tendency as a part of **your** life. One of the grossest sins that we commit is the invisible one of procrastination.

Procrastination is invisible because it does not even exist. You just do not act. You put things off. Tomorrow, we will go into action, will we not? Of course not. When tomorrow arrives, it will be today and today we are not going to do anything because we put that off until tomorrow.

If you would like to give up the anxiety and failure that accompany putting off things, you must first see how devastating this has always been to the fulfillment of your dreams.

Procrastination is the most widely scattered disease that lives among us. It is the one thing that every one of us has in common. Nothing new can happen until we give it up, because nothing new can happen until we begin to live in now moments, not tomorrow moments.

A procrastinator is a non-doer. A non-doer soon becomes a critic. A critic is a spectator of things being done in other people's lives and an expert in how someone else should have done something. This person is an expert in how they would have done it, providing they ever did anything, but they do not do anything, until tomorrow.

INTO ACTION
Let a Winner Lead the Way

Critics are the bystanders that life is always waving to as it passes them by. Show me a critic. I will show you a procrastinator.

The person who goes into action does not have time, nor the energy, nor the desire to criticize, condemn or judge.

There are many, many ways to procrastinate. One of the busiest men I have ever known is a procrastination specialist. He is always busy tracing down deals, talking about how much he has to do. He will drive half way across town to have a cup of coffee with you and talk about all kinds of things to do.

Every time I see him, he has something else for me to do. He has a hospital call for me to make or some new way of implementing something that I have not yet implemented. He is especially good at finding someone for me to help who does not want my help or the help of any other person.

My friend has started a zillion projects and I do not think he has ever finished one.

Now, I am not criticizing him. I love him dearly. I understand the inner tension, the anxiety, the fear, the low self-esteem, the sense of impending doom, because he knows that his projects are never ever going to be finished. They will never be completed simply because he never begins them. How can you complete something if you do not start? You just cannot.

... AND THAT'S THE WAY IT REALLY IS!

My friend will get started with his life right away, tomorrow, if it ever gets here and when it gets here he will not start ... for it will be today.

You can do anything you set your mind to do. You have everything necessary to achieve your goals, whether you believe it or not, but only if you go into action. If you put things off to a future time, you are freezing yourself, causing the fluid of motion to become the ice of stagnation and non-motion.

Procrastination is inertia. It is resistance to action, change or motion. Have you ever tried to push a stalled automobile? Until you get its huge mass moving you meet with great resistance, but once this mass starts to move, the automobile rolls easily, does it not? So it is with you. Overcoming resistance is the overcoming of inertia, and **action** is the catalyst that starts the automobile rolling.

If you will look at every one of your goals, you will see **an action possibility** that exists for you. If you would demonstrate your goals, you must take that action.

Procrastination, which has held us all back, has been born of fear and that fear must be conquered. It can be conquered if you act **without hesitation**. If you go into action, the lion of terror will be reduced to an ant of equanimity.

INTO ACTION
Let a Winner Lead the Way

To paraphrase from Og Mandino. "I will act now. I will awaken in the morning and I will say to myself, this is a day that I will go into action. If I am tempted to quit, I will begin again."

From time to time, in my life, I have resisted going into action. I found myself not feeling fulfilled. Something was lacking. Something was wrong. The **moment** I took the slightest step into action, the feeling changed. I felt alive again. Do not hesitate to **do something!** Start to apply these principles in your life. Go into action! The excitement you generate for yourself will astound you.

INTO ACTION
Let a Winner Lead the Way

I believe in you! I know you can achieve greatness in your life, if you will but go into action. If you do not yet believe in yourself, let my belief in you, carry you through. Surround yourself with like minded people who can join you in supporting your success. Follow your ACTION, with PERSISTENCE, and the world will be yours!

... And That's The Way It REALLY Is!

Jack Boland